AF529574

Lilly's Life Journal

Geetha Rani

Qurate
quratebooks.com

Lilly's Life Journal
Geetha Rani

© Geetha Rani

Published in 2024

© Published by

qurate
quratebooks.com

Qurate Books Pvt. Ltd.
Goa 403523, India
www.quratebooks.com
Tel: 1800-210-6527, Email: info@quratebooks.com

All rights reserved
No part of this publication may be reproduced, stored in a retrieval system, or transmitted in any form or by any means, electronic, mechanical, photocopying, recording or otherwise, without the prior permission of the author.

ISBN: 978-93-58985-02-3

"In the story, there are two narrators. One is Lilly herself, telling about her past and how she started her journey. The other is the author, narrating Lilly's story."

Just like an onion, human nature reveals itself layer by layer, often bringing tears as we peel it back. Each layer holds something new—sometimes it contrasts with the others, sometimes it aligns. Yet, we rarely stop to think about the consequences of revealing these layers or the situations we might create for others in the process. All we care about is how satisfied or happy we are in the current moment, how much we gain, and how far we advance in the game of life. We call it survival.

Once, survival was simple. It was about staying alive in critical circumstances, ensuring we had food at the right time, and protecting ourselves from danger. But over time, survival has shifted into something entirely different. Now, it's not just about living—it's about competing, achieving, and proving. It's about ensuring we don't lose, no matter the cost. The meaning of survival has evolved, shaped by our desires, fears, and the complexities of the modern world.

As someone who once surrendered to fears, insecurities, and self-doubt, I am embarking on my survival journey today. This is not a fight against the world but a path inward—a quest to confront the layers I've built over time. These layers, forged by hesitation and shaped by past failures, have shielded me but also held me back. Now, it's time to peel them away.

Survival, I've come to understand, is not just about enduring—it's about reclaiming. It's about reclaiming the strength hidden beneath fear, the clarity buried under self-doubt, and the confidence lost to insecurities. This journey is about becoming whole, not by escaping what I've been through, but by facing it and allowing it to shape a version of myself that's free from the weight of constant validation and fear of failure. It's about choosing to truly live, not merely exist.

I'm Lillyput, though most people call me Lilly. My survival journey began when I was just 9 years old—a time when childhood should be filled with innocence and wonder. But for me, life took a different turn. I was thrust into a reality that forced me to grow up too soon, leaving behind the carefree days that others my age still enjoyed. Wondering what could strip away innocence so early? So was I, and that question became the starting point of my journey.

It wasn't a stranger who threatened me—it was someone I knew. Someone I trusted. A family friend. Someone I thought would always protect me. I was at their house one afternoon, and it all happened so suddenly, so unexpectedly. We were alone in a room when they started to talk to me in a way that made my skin crawl. At first, I thought maybe I misunderstood, but as they came closer, the words started to feel less like conversation and more like a warning. "If you tell anyone, no one will believe you," they said. The chill in their voice cut through me. I froze.

I couldn't process what was happening. How could someone I knew—someone who had been a part of my life—be capable of making me feel so small and vulnerable? My mind raced, but my body stayed still, paralyzed by fear. I knew I had to find a way out, but I didn't know how to escape without making things worse. I didn't know how to fight back against someone who had once been a friend, someone I thought I could trust.

That moment shattered something inside me. Afterward, I walked away, but I wasn't the same. I felt betrayed—not just by that person, but by the world. How could someone I thought I could trust do this to me? I felt dirty, confused, and ashamed. I had always believed that people close to me were safe, that I could count on them. But that belief was ripped away, leaving me to grapple with the darkness that followed.

The hardest part wasn't just the fear or the shame. It was the confusion that followed—how to make sense of something that didn't fit into the life I thought I knew. I started questioning everything—my relationships, my boundaries, my trust. I didn't know who to turn to, or how to explain what happened. How could I tell someone that the person I trusted had hurt me?

Over time, I began to see that this moment didn't have to define me. It changed me, yes, but I didn't want it to control me. I had to learn to rebuild—my trust, my confidence, and most importantly, my sense of self. It wasn't easy, and the scars stayed with me, but I learned that survival wasn't just about avoiding danger. It was about reclaiming my power, facing my fear, and slowly learning to trust again.

That moment marked the beginning of my survival journey. Not just surviving in the physical sense, but surviving emotionally, mentally, and spiritually. It's been a long road, but I've learned that the true strength comes from facing the darkness, learning from it, and finding the courage to move forward—one step at a time.

As the days passed, I found myself sinking deeper into that dark place. The confusion, the insecurities, and the fear weren't just passing feelings anymore—they were becoming a part of who I was. I was lost in a maze of my own mind, consumed by questions I couldn't answer. "Why did this happen to me?" "What did I do wrong?" "How could I have been so naive?" These questions swirled inside me, like a storm that wouldn't stop. There was no peace, no moment of calm. Just a constant battle between my thoughts and emotions.

And then there was the self-hate. A deep, gnawing feeling that I couldn't shake. I hated myself for not seeing the signs, for trusting someone who didn't deserve it. I hated myself for allowing this to happen, for not fighting back harder, for not screaming loud enough, for not doing anything that could have stopped it. It wasn't just about what they did to me—it was about what I thought I should have done, how I blamed myself for being weak, for being so easily taken advantage of.

I began to believe that maybe I deserved it—that somehow, this was my punishment, my consequence for being too trusting, too naive. The world felt like a cruel place, and I hated myself for letting it get to this point. I couldn't shake the thought that I should have been smarter, stronger, more capable of protecting myself. Every time I thought about that day, I felt the weight of the regret pressing on my chest. Why did I let this happen? Why didn't I fight harder?

With all this swirling inside me, I started to accept the darkest path. I told myself that this was who I was now—someone broken, someone scarred. The questions didn't stop, but I didn't seek answers anymore. I was too tired, too numb. There was no sense in trying to find a way out because I had already convinced myself that this was where I was meant to be. I wasn't going to heal. I wasn't going to overcome. I was just going to exist in this space, stuck in the aftermath of something that wasn't my fault, but somehow, I felt like it was.

I became resentful—not just of the person who hurt me, but of myself for letting it happen. I let the hate fester, thinking that maybe, just maybe, if I hated myself enough, the pain would go away. If I blamed myself enough, I would be able to bury the anger, the shame, the hurt. But the truth was, the hate didn't heal anything—it only made it worse. The more I hated myself, the more I sank deeper into the darkness.

I was walking a path I never wanted, filled with self-doubt and regret, but for a long time, I didn't know how to turn back. I didn't know how to reclaim the parts of me that felt lost.

I remember a time when I tried to tell someone, anyone, about what I was going through. I was desperate to be heard, to make them understand the pain that was eating me up inside. I thought if I just spoke the words, if I just opened up, someone would listen and offer me the comfort I so desperately needed.

But instead of hearing me, they turned their attention to everything that had nothing to do with the pain I was carrying. "Why are you talking like that?" they asked, mocking the tone of my voice, as if the way I spoke was more important than the story I was trying to tell. "You sound so strange," they said, making me feel like there was something wrong with the way I was expressing myself. They didn't see the tears I was holding back or the struggle behind my words. They only saw a voice they thought was too much or too little, a voice that didn't fit their expectations.

And then there were the comments about my appearance—my color, my size, the way I looked. "You're too dark," they laughed, like it was a joke. "You should lose some weight," they'd say, as if I didn't already feel the weight of my own body every single day. The looks of disapproval, the eye rolls when I walked into a room, the whispers when I wasn't around—they all made me feel invisible, like my worth was tied to how I looked, not who I was.

I had poured my heart out, hoping for empathy, but instead, I was met with ridicule. It was like my words didn't matter, my feelings didn't matter—only the things that were easy to point out about me, the things I couldn't change, became the focal point. It didn't matter that I was hurting; it didn't matter that I was crying for help. What mattered to them was how I spoke, how I looked, how I sounded.

It was in that moment that I learned the hard truth: sometimes, people don't want to understand. They don't want to listen to your pain—they just want to criticize, to make you feel smaller so they don't have to confront their own insecurities. I started to believe that maybe I wasn't worth listening to. Maybe my pain wasn't real enough for them to care. And with every unkind word, every cruel joke about my body, my voice, and my color, I sank further into myself, retreating even deeper into the darkness.

The more they laughed, the more I felt like I was drowning. The more I tried to explain, the more I felt like I was disappearing. I stopped talking about it. I stopped trying to share what I was going through. It was easier to just keep it inside and hide the hurt, to let the darkness consume me. Because when you're not heard, when your pain is mocked, you start to think that maybe you deserve to be invisible.

After hearing the mockery, the shame, and the ridicule day after day, it became harder and harder for me to even express an emotion. At first, I tried to fight it, tried to hold on to some semblance of who I used to be. I tried to cry, to scream, to show the world that I was hurt. But every time I did, it was met with dismissal, with jokes at my expense. It was like my pain had become a performance, and no one cared enough to be an audience.

Slowly, I learned to close off. I stopped showing my emotions, stopped letting anyone see my vulnerability. I built walls around myself, thick walls that I thought would protect me from the world's cruelty. But the more I shut down, the more distant I became from everything I used to feel. I stopped crying. I stopped being angry. I stopped caring about anything at all. The pain I had carried for so long became too exhausting, and in my attempt to survive, I just... stopped feeling.

It wasn't a conscious choice, not at first. It was more like an automatic reaction to the constant judgment. When you're constantly told that who you are isn't good enough, that you're too much or not enough, it starts to wear you down. Eventually, you reach a point where you just can't process it anymore. I couldn't feel the sharp sting of pain anymore because I had numbed myself to it. I couldn't feel the anger I wanted to release because I had buried it so deep inside. I couldn't even feel the sadness. Everything turned into a dull, empty gray.

The worst part was that I didn't even notice it happening at first. It was like a slow fade, like the colors of my emotions were being washed away, one by one, until everything was just... neutral. My thoughts were quieter. My heart felt still. There was no joy, no sorrow, no excitement, no anger—just a hollow emptiness that I had to carry with me every day. It was like I was standing outside of myself, watching the world continue while I stood still, unable to connect to anything or anyone.

This neutral state, this emotional void, became my shield. It was safer to feel nothing than to risk feeling anything at all. It was easier to exist in this numb space than to face the hurt, the anger, or the shame that had taken root deep inside of me. I had conditioned myself to not care, because caring meant feeling—and feeling meant getting hurt again.

But the hardest part of this numbness was that it wasn't just a defense. It wasn't just a way to survive. Over time, it became my reality. I had stopped fighting for myself, stopped hoping for things to get better. I had stopped believing that I could feel again, that I deserved to feel again. And so, I remained in this emotional stasis, stuck in a place where nothing really mattered anymore. It was a lonely, suffocating place to be. But at least it was quiet. And sometimes, that was all I could ask for.

Just when I thought I had found a way to numb the world around me, life had a way of reminding me that the silence was never truly peaceful. The quiet that I had created to shield myself from the world was suddenly shattered by the constant noise of my parents' arguments. It started off small—little disagreements here and there, but soon it became a never-ending storm. It felt like there was no escaping it. Every day, I would come home, hoping for peace, for a moment where I could just breathe, but all I found was shouting, blaming, and hurtful words thrown at each other.

Their fights didn't just fill the house – they filled my mind. It was like being trapped in the middle of a battle, where neither side was fighting for me, but for their own egos. I tried to ignore it at first, to retreat further into my emotional silence, but it wasn't that easy. I could hear everything. Their voices rising, the anger in their words, the way they spoke to each other like they were enemies. And I couldn't shut it out anymore. It felt like my home, the one place that should have been safe, was the epicenter of chaos.

The constant tension in the air was suffocating. I would try to focus on my studies, my silence, anything that could distract me, but the anger and frustration that filled the house seeped into me. I began to feel like I was walking on eggshells, never knowing when the next fight would break out, or what it would be about this time. It was exhausting. It was draining. And it made everything inside me feel heavier, more overwhelming.

What made it worse was that I couldn't express my feelings. I was already numb from years of shaming, and now, the emotional toll of the constant fighting at home was like another weight on top of the pile. Every argument made me feel even more invisible. I couldn't talk to my parents about how I felt because it felt like they were too lost in their own pain and anger to care about mine. I wasn't even sure how to express what I was feeling anymore – my own emotions had become foreign to me.

The mental health toll was real, though. The stress, the anxiety, the constant feeling of being trapped in an environment that was supposed to offer comfort—it all started to take its toll on my mind. I began to feel like I was sinking deeper into the darkness, like every day was one more step further away from the person I used to be. The fighting made me feel small, unimportant. I began to internalize the chaos, believing that somehow I was the cause of it, that if I were different, they wouldn't be fighting. I didn't understand how to fix things, but I blamed myself anyway.

I would sit in my room, headphones on, trying to block out the noise. But even with music blaring, I couldn't escape the weight of it. The shouting echoed in my ears, filling every empty space I tried to create. The quietness I had worked so hard to cultivate was shattered once again, replaced by the constant buzz of tension and anger. I felt like I was suffocating, caught in a cycle that I couldn't break.

It wasn't just the noise that hurt. It was the realization that I couldn't change it. No matter how much I wanted peace, no matter how much I wanted the fighting to stop, it felt like my hands were tied. I had already lost so much of myself, and now, it felt like the last shred of safety and stability I had was crumbling away. And yet, no one saw it—no one saw how this constant chaos was eating me alive. I was trapped in my own home, in my own mind, with no way out.

I tried to end it. More than once. I thought that maybe, just maybe, if I could escape this pain, if I could just stop existing, it would all go away. The numbness, the fear, the loneliness—it would end. I wouldn't have to carry the weight of everything anymore. I could stop pretending to be okay when I was falling apart inside. I thought maybe, just maybe, giving up would be my release.

But every time I tried, something stopped me. A fleeting moment of clarity, a thought that maybe I could fight a little longer, a faint whisper telling me that it wasn't the answer, that this wasn't the way out. I would fail at giving up, and then I would blame myself. I would lie there, in the aftermath, feeling even worse than before. Not only was I still stuck in this painful, dark place, but now I felt like I wasn't even good enough at ending it all. I couldn't even do that right.

I hated myself for it. I blamed myself for not having the courage to make the pain stop. The one thing I thought would finally release me from this endless cycle of misery was something I couldn't even follow through with. It made me feel more broken, more unworthy of love or compassion. If I couldn't even give up on my own life, what did that say about me? Why was I so pathetic, so weak, that I couldn't even succeed in ending the suffocating silence inside me?

It wasn't the failure of the attempts that hurt the most, though. It was the realization that even in my darkest moments, I couldn't escape the emptiness. I couldn't escape the thoughts that always circled back to the same place: that no matter how much I tried to disappear, I was still here. And I hated it.

Each time I tried to let go, each time I failed, it felt like the universe was mocking me. I couldn't even leave this world without feeling like I wasn't good enough for it. I wasn't good enough to even die in peace. And that thought, that belief, that I couldn't even escape my own pain—it tore me apart more than anything else. I became convinced that there was no way out, no way forward. I wasn't worth saving.

But in some strange way, even though I failed, I kept existing. I kept waking up every day, going through the motions, pretending that I had it all together. And the more I failed to give up, the more I started to realize that maybe, just maybe, I was still fighting. I wasn't sure what I was fighting for yet, but I was still here. And somewhere deep inside, that small voice—the one I had tried to silence so many times—was telling me that it wasn't too late to find a way out, to find a way to heal.

It wasn't until I met Kathey that I started to feel like maybe—just maybe—I wasn't alone in all this. I had always believed that I was the only one who carried this darkness, this pain that weighed so heavily on me. But Kathey, with her soft eyes and gentle presence, was different. She never judged me. She didn't turn away when I shared the deepest parts of my soul, parts I had hidden for so long, afraid of what others might think. When I opened up to her, when I poured out the fear, the confusion, the anger, the guilt, she didn't flinch. She didn't tell me to stop feeling, didn't tell me to get over it. She just listened.

And then, one day, she hugged me. It wasn't the kind of hug that promised to fix things or make everything better—it was the kind of hug that told me she understood, that she cared, that I didn't have to carry this burden alone. In that moment, I felt a weight lift off me, even if it was only for a second. For the first time in what felt like forever, I felt seen. I felt like maybe someone—just one person—actually understood the hell I was going through.

But the thing that shook me, that really left me questioning everything, came a few days later. I found Kathey sitting by herself in a corner of the park near our school, her shoulders shaking as she cried. At first, I thought it was just another one of those random moments of sadness that we all have. But there was something different about the way she cried—like she had been holding it in for too long, like she had reached a breaking point.

I walked over to her, my heart heavy with worry, and asked, "Kathey, what happened? Why are you crying?" She looked up at me, her face pale and tired, and for a moment, she hesitated, like she wasn't sure if she could trust me with her pain. But then, with a deep breath, she opened up.

"I've been going through a lot," she said, her voice cracking. "Things at home, things with my family, my own thoughts. I don't know... I just feel lost."

As she spoke, my mind raced. She described feelings of loneliness, fear, confusion, and emotional numbness—all the things I had gone through. It felt like I was hearing my own story, just in someone else's voice. She had suffered in silence, just like I had. She had battled with the same feelings of self-doubt, the same internal struggle to keep fighting even when she felt like giving up.

"Kathey," I said, my voice barely a whisper, "this... this is just like what I've been going through. The fights at home, the loneliness, the confusion, the numbness..." I felt a sudden chill run through me as the realization sank in. How could this be? How could she be going through the exact same thing I had? For the longest time, I had wondered why this was happening to me. Why I was the one who was always suffering, who always seemed to be stuck in this darkness. But now, sitting there with Kathey, I saw that these feelings, this pain—it wasn't just mine. It wasn't something unique to me. There were others, like Kathey, who had experienced the same things, who had been carrying their own burdens in silence.

It was like a bombshell dropped in my mind. For years, I had thought I was the only one—alone in my struggles, isolated in my pain. But Kathey's confession made me realize that there were others out there, living with the same quiet anguish. And suddenly, my world felt both smaller and bigger at the same time. Smaller, because it was no longer just my pain—it was shared by others. But bigger, because I was now faced with the question: how many others like Kathey were out there? How many people had suffered in silence, just like I had?

I was left in shock, confused by this realization. How had I never known? How had I been so blinded to the fact that these things happened to others too? Why had I always felt like the victim, the one who was cursed to endure this? Maybe it wasn't just me after all. Maybe, in some strange way, we were all walking similar paths, carrying similar burdens. And for the first time, I realized that maybe I wasn't as alone as I thought.

Things took a darker turn for Kathey when her parents, who had always been a pillar of support for her, suddenly turned their backs on her. It was over something she had no control over, something that wasn't even her fault. Someone, someone from her school or neighborhood, had spread a lie about her. The details didn't even matter to her anymore. All that mattered was the fact that her parents believed the lie without questioning her, without listening to her side of the story.

They had always trusted her, had always seen her as the strong, responsible one. But now, that trust was shattered in an instant. They blamed her for something that wasn't hers to bear. The weight of their accusations hit her like a blow to the chest, knocking all the air out of her. She tried to explain, to make them see the truth, but they were too caught up in their own beliefs, in the words of someone else. And no matter how hard she tried, no matter how many times she pleaded, they just didn't listen.

The worst part was the feeling of betrayal. She had never imagined that her own parents would doubt her, would stand on the other side when she needed them the most. And with that, the loneliness that had always lingered in her heart grew even more unbearable.

Kathey had always been there for me, listening to my pain, offering comfort when I needed it most. She was the one who had been my rock, my strength when I felt like I couldn't go on. But now, in her own brokenness, she was lost. She was still fighting her demons, but now she had no one to turn to.

I watched her as she sank deeper into herself. She tried to put on a brave face, tried to continue being the friend I needed her to be, but I could see it—the cracks beneath her smile, the emptiness in her eyes. She couldn't hold it together anymore. She couldn't console me when she needed comfort herself.

And then, one day, it happened. Kathey gave up. She decided she couldn't keep going. It wasn't that she didn't care about life anymore—it was that life had become too much to handle, and there was no escape from the pain. She felt like a stranger in her own home, like the walls that had once supported her were now closing in on her. And no matter how much she tried to reach out, no one heard her cries.

She left us. Left the world. And all I could think was, "Why didn't I see it? Why didn't I realize that she was as lost as I was? Why didn't I help her the way she helped me?" The guilt consumed me. I felt like I had failed her, just like everyone else in her life had. She had been the one who understood me, who listened without judgment, who held me when I cried. But when it was her turn to break down, when she needed someone the most, I wasn't there for her in the way she needed me to be.

The loss of Kathey shattered something deep inside me. I didn't know how to handle it, how to process the grief, the guilt, the anger. All I knew was that I felt more alone than I had ever felt before. I wondered if anyone could understand this kind of pain—the kind that comes from losing someone who was your everything, who made you feel seen when the rest of the world had looked away.

And it made me realize, more than ever, that none of us are truly alone in our struggles. Kathey and I, we had been walking similar paths, carrying similar burdens, but we couldn't save each other. We couldn't rescue one another from the pain that had consumed us both.

The loss of Kathey should have broken me completely, but instead, something inside me shifted. It was like a spark, a flicker of strength that ignited within me, telling me that I had to keep going. I couldn't give up. Not now. Not after everything. Kathey had fought her demons in silence, and though I couldn't save her, I could honor her by surviving, by finding my own way through the darkness.

But as much as I tried to push forward, as much as I tried to find that strength, the chaos in my life never let up. It was as if every day brought something new to tear me down. The fights at home, the constant feeling of being misunderstood, the noise, the pressure, the never-ending struggle—it all weighed on me like a hundred-pound stone.

I became trapped between two worlds. On one side, I saw life, and I felt this tiny, fragile hope flickering within me, urging me to keep going, to stay alive. But on the other side, there was death—death in the sense of giving up, of surrendering to the pain, of choosing to leave it all behind and never have to face the chaos again. It was a battle, a constant fight between these two forces, and it tore me apart every single day.

In the quiet of my room, when everything around me seemed to stop, I would dwell in myself. I would sit in the silence, my thoughts swirling like a storm, and I would wonder if it was all worth it. The fight, the pain, the exhaustion. Was it even worth trying anymore?

But then there would be moments when the thoughts of giving up crept in. The fear of facing another day, the fear of never escaping the constant noise in my head, the fear of the uncertainty of everything—it all became too much. And I would be stuck, paralyzed in this constant tug-of-war between wanting to live and wanting to escape. It was like I was standing on the edge of a cliff, not knowing if I should jump or turn around and walk back into the chaos.

Mentally, I was unraveling. The confusion, the fear, the self-doubt—it consumed me. Every word, every action, every little thing around me felt like a trigger, pushing me further into the abyss of my thoughts. I began to lose track of time, of my own sense of reality. It was like I was existing, but not really living. Like I was floating in between two worlds, unable to choose which path to take.

I found myself questioning everything—my worth, my purpose, my future. And most of all, I questioned whether I was even capable of surviving this. The constant battle between life and death, between holding on and letting go, had left me mentally drained. My mind was a maze of fear, confusion, and anger, and no matter how hard I tried to find my way out, I kept getting lost in it.

And yet, despite all of this, there was something deep within me that refused to let go completely. Even when I felt like I was drowning in my own thoughts, there was a flicker of hope, however small, that kept me tethered to life. It was as if my soul was clinging to the idea that maybe, just maybe, things could get better. But the fear was always there, lurking in the shadows, reminding me how fragile everything was.

Every day felt like a fight—one I wasn't sure I could win. But I kept fighting anyway. I didn't know how long I could hold on, but I knew that, for now, I had to keep going. The chaos, the fear, the pain—it all lived inside me, and no matter how hard I tried to escape it, it was always there, a part of me. And the hardest part was not knowing how to break free from it.

It was during one of those days when I was drowning in my thoughts, trying to make sense of the mess inside my head, that I stumbled upon something online—something that caught my attention in the midst of all the chaos. It was a website that offered something unique: the ability to send a letter to your future self. You could schedule a message to be delivered to you at some point in the future, a snapshot of who you were, what you were going through, and what you hoped for.

At first, I thought it was just another gimmick, another one of those "feel-good" websites that promised to fix everything with a few inspirational words. But there was something about the idea of writing to my future self that felt different. It felt real. It felt like a chance to talk to someone—someone who might understand the pain, the fear, and the confusion that had taken over my life.

I decided to give it a try. I sat down in front of my computer, my fingers hovering over the keyboard as I thought about what I wanted to say. It wasn't easy. I had so many thoughts, so many emotions swirling inside me, but I knew that I needed to say something—to give myself a voice in a time when I felt like no one was listening.

I wrote about everything I had been through—the abuse, the betrayal, the loneliness, the fear, and the moments when I felt like giving up. I talked about how the world had seemed to turn its back on me, and how I was stuck in a constant battle between life and death. I told my future self how hard it was to keep going, how much I wanted to escape the pain and find peace, but how something deep inside me refused to let go completely.

But more than anything, I wished for one thing: a friend. Not just any friend, but a friend who would truly understand me, who would accept me for who I was, flaws and all. A friend who would be there in the darkest of times, who wouldn't turn their back on me when the going got tough. I wished for someone who would listen without judgment, who would offer comfort when I felt like I was drowning in my own thoughts.

I wrote to myself, telling the future me that I was holding on to whatever hope I could find, even on the darkest days. I wrote about the tiny moments of light I was holding on to, the small fragments of hope that still managed to flicker through the cracks of my despair. I didn't know what the future held, but I promised myself that I would keep going, one day at a time, even when it felt like everything was falling apart.

And then, I scheduled the letter to be sent to me in ten years. A message from the past to the future. A reminder of where I was, what I had gone through, and the hope that I was still holding on to, even when it felt like hope had abandoned me.

I didn't know if I would ever have a chance to read that letter, if I would even be around to see it. But I wrote it anyway. Because somehow, just writing it down—putting my thoughts, my fears, my wishes into words—made me feel a little less alone. And maybe, just maybe, in ten years, I would look back at that letter and see how far I had come. Or maybe I would read it and see that I had finally found the strength to let go of the pain. Either way, I was holding on to the hope that the future could be different—that I could be different.

[The Letter]

Dear Future Me,

I don't know what's going on in your life right now, or if you've found some kind of peace, but I'm writing to you because right now, I can't see a way out. I don't even know how to explain what I'm feeling. It's all too much, and I can't seem to make sense of any of it. I feel lost, confused, and everything around me feels like it's falling apart.

I'm tired of this pain, tired of carrying all of it. It's like this heavy weight inside me, and no matter what I do, I can't shake it. I've tried pretending everything is fine, tried to act like I'm okay, but I'm not. I'm really not. I don't think anyone sees how much I'm hurting. And honestly, I don't know if I can keep going like this.

Lately, I've been thinking about Kathey a lot. She was the only one who truly listened to me, the only one who seemed to care. I still remember how she would sit with me when no one else would, how she would just hug me when I needed it the most. She was the one who didn't judge me for what I was going through. When everything seemed too much, she was there to help me carry the weight.

But now she's gone. Kathey isn't here anymore. She… she took her own life, and I don't even know how to process that. How could someone who helped me, who was there for me, feel so alone that she thought there was no way out? I still hear her voice in my head sometimes, and I wish, I wish I could have done something, anything, to save her.

Her death feels like a punch to my gut. It's so painful, and yet, it's made everything so much worse. It makes me question everything, makes me wonder if there's any hope left for me too. If Kathey couldn't make it through, then how can I? I feel like I'm standing at the edge, looking into the abyss, and I don't know how much longer I can stay here.

I keep thinking about how much I miss her, and how much I wish I had a friend like Kathey now. Someone who could listen to me without judgment. Someone who would hug me when I feel like the world is too cold. Someone who would stay by my side, no matter how dark things get. I don't think I can go on without someone like that. I don't know how to survive this emptiness.

I'm writing this to you, Future Me, hoping that by the time you read this, things will be different. I hope that you've found peace, and I hope that you have the kind of friendship I've been searching for. A friend who understands, who doesn't turn away when things get hard, who won't judge me for my brokenness. I need that now more than ever.

If you're reading this, Future Me, I hope that you've found a way to heal, to accept yourself, and to make sense of all the pain. I hope that you've found the strength to keep going. Because right now, I don't know if I have it in me to keep going. I don't know if I'll ever feel whole again, but I'm holding on to this tiny thread of hope that one day I will.

I just want to know that it will get better. I just want to know that I'm not alone in this fight.

With all the pain,

Lilly

And I sent the mail with the hope that one day I'll read it.

The next morning, after writing the letter to my future self, something inside me felt lighter. It was as if I had shared my deepest, darkest thoughts with someone, even though it was just a letter. I slept better that night, the weight of everything feeling a little less heavy. For the first time in a long while, I allowed myself to rest.

The following day, as I walked to school, something unexpected happened. I was lost in my own thoughts, still trying to make sense of everything that had happened in the last few days, when suddenly, I collided with someone. The impact was enough to knock me off balance, and I stumbled slightly. I looked up, startled, to see a boy about my age standing there, equally surprised by the accident.

We both stood still for a second, processing what had just happened, before we both muttered, "Sorry!" at the same time.

I looked at him, a little dazed, and noticed he had a casual air about him. There was something about him that caught my attention—something different. "Are you from this school?" I asked, trying to make sense of who he was.

He seemed to think for a moment before shaking his head. "Nah, I'm not from here," he replied with a shrug. "I don't really go to school. I'm... kind of... from the streets."

I blinked, caught off guard by his response. "What do you mean? You don't go to school?" I asked, a little unsure how to react.

He met my gaze and said, "I'm an orphan. No parents, no guardians. Just me." His voice was steady, but there was a quiet strength in it. He didn't seem ashamed of what he was saying, but it also didn't sound like he was bragging about it either. It was just... the truth.

"Wow," I whispered, trying to process this new information. "I've never met anyone like you before."

He gave a small, almost amused smile. "Yeah, people usually don't know how to react. But that's how it is. I've learned to live on my own." He paused for a moment before adding, "It's not as bad as it sounds. I've gotten by."

I stood there for a moment, trying to understand. Then, before I could say anything else, he seemed to read my mind and added quickly, "But don't look at me with that pity, alright?"

I was taken aback. "Pity? I wasn't—" I started, but he cut me off with a soft chuckle.

"I don't need sympathy," Max said, his tone firm but not unkind. "I'm not asking for anyone's charity. I've been through a lot, sure, but I don't want people treating me any differently. I'm still just a regular guy."

I nodded slowly, starting to understand. There was something raw about the way he spoke—no pretensions, no dramatization. It felt like he had been through his own battles but didn't want anyone to see him as fragile or broken.

"Alright, buddy," I said, offering a slight smile. "No pity. I'll treat you like a normal guy."

Max's eyes softened, and a small grin spread across his face. "That's better," he said, and for a brief moment, it felt like a genuine connection had been made between us.

In that brief exchange, I felt something shift. It wasn't much, but it was enough to make me feel like maybe, just maybe, things could change. For the first time in a long while, I didn't feel quite as alone. But that's just for a second, after walking forward a while I again dwelled into my own thoughts.

[Narration by author]

At school, Lilly found herself once again at the center of unwanted attention. Her classmates didn't need much of a reason; sometimes it was her frizzy hair, sometimes the color of her skin, and sometimes just the way she spoke. The whispers, the giggles, and the casual comments weren't new, but they still cut deep.

"Did you see what she's wearing today? So outdated," someone sneered, loud enough for Lilly to hear.

Another added with a smirk, "Maybe she thinks it's cool to look... different."

Lilly had learned not to react. Each remark piled onto the invisible wall she'd built around herself, a wall that kept her emotions locked away. She wouldn't cry, wouldn't lash out—she just stared ahead, her expression blank.

"Neutral. Stay neutral," she told herself, repeating the mantra like a shield against their words. She had learned to accept this reality, at least for the moment. It was easier to retreat into her shell than to fight a battle she knew she couldn't win.

When the school day finally ended, Lilly walked home, her head bowed. She entered the house only to find her parents locked in yet another argument. Their voices carried through the walls, sharp and angry, filling every corner of the home with tension.

"Why don't you ever listen to me?" her mother's voice echoed.

"You're the one who never understands!" her father shot back.

Lilly's room, her sanctuary, felt oppressive in the face of the chaos. She tried to focus on her studies, but the shouting broke through her concentration like shattering glass. Exhausted, she closed her books and decided to escape.

Climbing the stairs to the terrace, Lilly felt the weight of the day pressing down on her shoulders. As she stepped onto the open space, the evening breeze greeted her, a brief respite from the suffocating atmosphere below.

She walked to the edge and leaned against the railing, her eyes fixed on the horizon. The setting sun painted the sky in hues of orange and gold, its beauty contrasting sharply with the turmoil inside her.

For the first time that day, Lilly allowed herself to breathe deeply. Watching the sun slowly sink, she felt a small flicker of peace—fragile and fleeting, but enough to keep her standing. The silence of the terrace was a stark contrast to the noise of her life, and for that brief moment, it was enough.

As Lilly stood on the terrace, soaking in the calming hues of the sunset, a faint sound began to creep into her sanctuary. At first, it was barely noticeable—a muffled echo of voices. But soon, the sounds grew louder, piercing through the peace she had found just moments ago.

Her parents' argument had escalated again, their voices now reaching the terrace. Each word was sharp, filled with anger and blame, cutting through the evening air.

"I've had enough of this nonsense!" her father's voice boomed.

"Then maybe you should leave if you can't handle it!" her mother retaliated, her tone equally fierce.

Lilly clenched the railing tightly, her knuckles turning white. She could feel the tension rising in her chest, a storm brewing inside her. The shouting felt like a hammer, striking repeatedly, shattering any semblance of calm she had managed to build.

She squeezed her eyes shut, as tightly as she could, trying to block out the noise. It didn't help. The words seeped in, louder and sharper, like they were echoing inside her head. Her breathing grew heavier, and her jaw tightened as if bracing against an unseen blow.

For a moment, it felt like she was about to lose control, the patience she had carefully held onto all day slipping away.

"Stop... please stop," she whispered to herself, her voice trembling. But the shouting continued, relentless and deafening, drowning her quiet plea.

She pressed her palms against her ears, shutting her eyes even tighter, as if trying to physically push the chaos away. The terrace, once a refuge, now felt as suffocating as the rest of her life. The peaceful sunset blurred behind her closed eyelids, overtaken by the darkness she was desperately trying to escape.

As Lilly stood frozen, her eyes tightly shut and hands pressed against her ears, a sudden sensation startled her—a gentle hand on her shoulder. The unexpected touch broke through her storm of thoughts like a lightning strike, sending a jolt through her entire body.

She gasped sharply and jumped back instinctively, her eyes snapping open in alarm. Her heart raced as she turned to face whoever had disrupted her tense solitude.

"Whoa! Easy there," came a familiar voice, calm yet tinged with a hint of amusement.

It was Buddy.

He stood there, hands raised slightly in a gesture of peace, his face holding a small, reassuring smile. His presence was so unexpected that for a moment, Lilly was at a loss for words.

"Buddy?" she stammered, her voice shaky, still trying to process the sudden interruption. "What... what are you doing here?"

"I saw you up here," he said, shrugging casually. "Looked like you could use some company. Didn't mean to scare you, though. You okay?"

Lilly exhaled deeply, trying to calm her pounding heart. "You shouldn't sneak up on people like that," she said, though her tone was more tired than angry.

"Noted," Buddy replied with a playful smirk. "But seriously, you looked like you were about to implode. I figured you could use a distraction—or at least someone to remind you to breathe."

She stared at him for a moment, still shaken, but there was something oddly comforting about his presence. Despite the chaos around her, Buddy's carefree demeanor had a way of grounding her, even if just a little.

"Thanks... I guess," she muttered, brushing her hair away from her face.

Buddy took a step closer, leaning on the railing beside her. "Rough day?" he asked, glancing at her with a knowing look.

Lilly hesitated before nodding. "You could say that," she admitted quietly.

"Wanna talk about it?" he offered, his tone light but sincere.

She looked at him, unsure. The idea of opening up felt both daunting and strangely tempting. After a moment, she simply said, "Maybe later."

"Fair enough," Buddy replied, tilting his head toward the fading sunset. "For now, how about we just watch the sky? No talking, no overthinking—just this."

Lilly followed his gaze to the horizon, where the sun dipped lower, painting the sky in soft shades of orange and pink.

As the sun dipped below the horizon, its final rays casting a golden glow over the terrace, the chaos from the house below began to subside. The muffled shouting faded into an eerie quiet, leaving only the soft rustle of the evening breeze.

Lilly felt the tension in her chest ease slightly. She inhaled deeply, filling her lungs with the cool, calming air. Closing her eyes, she held the breath for a moment, letting the peace of the moment seep in. When she opened them again, the world seemed a little less suffocating.

"Feeling better now?" Buddy's voice broke the silence, gentle and steady.

She glanced at him, his silhouette framed against the twilight sky. His question didn't demand an answer, but she found herself nodding, a faint smile tugging at her lips.

Buddy straightened, brushing invisible dust from his pants. "Good," he said simply. "That's my cue then. I'll catch you later, Lilly."

Before she could say anything, he turned and began walking away, his steps light and deliberate. As he reached the stairs, he looked back over his shoulder and gave her a small wave.

"Bye for now," he said, a warm yet fleeting smile crossing his face before he disappeared down the steps.

Lilly stood there for a moment, staring at the empty spot where Buddy had just been. She didn't fully understand him—his sudden appearances, his carefree demeanor, his way of knowing exactly what she needed without asking. But tonight, his presence had been enough.

Turning back to the now-dark sky, Lilly took one last deep breath, letting the night air fill her with the promise of a quieter moment. For the first time in what felt like ages, she allowed herself to believe that maybe, just maybe, things could get better.

That night, for the first time in what felt like an eternity, Lilly lay in her bed with a strange sense of calm. The usual whirlwind of thoughts that kept her awake for hours seemed distant, almost muffled.

She pulled the blanket up to her chin, staring at the ceiling as a faint smile crept onto her lips. Her mind replayed Buddy's casual farewell and the soft sound of his footsteps fading away. It wasn't just his words but the way he carried a sense of ease, as if nothing in the world was too heavy to bear.

The muffled sounds of her parents' earlier argument had vanished entirely, leaving the house cloaked in silence. The only sound was the rhythmic ticking of the clock, a soothing reminder of time moving forward.

As her eyes grew heavy, Lilly allowed herself to surrender to the stillness. No questions haunted her, no regrets whispered in her ears. For once, she didn't feel the need to dissect her emotions or guard herself against the world.

Her breathing slowed, each inhale and exhale lulling her further into a peaceful slumber. Wrapped in the warmth of her bed, she drifted off, her mind free of its usual burdens.

That night, Lilly slept like a baby—undisturbed, unburdened, and, for the first time in years, at peace.

The next morning brought with it an unusual lightness in Lilly's heart. It was a school holiday, but instead of dreading another long day at home amidst her parents' chaos, she felt a glimmer of excitement. She quickly finished her breakfast, barely noticing the taste of her food, her mind elsewhere.

As she stepped out of the house, there was a subtle bounce in her step and a faint smile on her face—expressions that had been strangers to her for so long. She glanced around the familiar streets, her eyes scanning every corner.

"Where could he be?" she murmured under her breath, her heart racing with anticipation.

She wandered toward the small park near her house, her gaze darting among the benches and the swings, but Buddy was nowhere to be seen. A little disappointed, but still hopeful, she turned and started walking toward the school road, even though it was closed for the day.

On the way, she passed the little tea stall where groups of people usually gathered to chat. She hesitated for a moment, looking around, half expecting to see Buddy leaning casually against a wall or sitting on the pavement with that relaxed demeanor of his.

But he wasn't there.

As she continued her search, Lilly's joy began to mingle with a hint of nervousness. What if he doesn't come today? What if yesterday was just a one-time thing?

Her steps slowed as she reached the crossroads near the school gate. She stood there for a moment, looking in every direction, her heart sinking a little.

But then, she shook her head, determined not to let the hope fade. "Maybe he'll show up later," she thought, trying to reassure herself.

With a sigh, she turned around and began walking back home, her eyes still scanning the streets as if Buddy might suddenly appear around the next corner.

Lilly walked back home, her steps slow and heavy, the disappointment of the day weighing her down. Reaching the front door, she paused, glancing up at the dimming sky. The warm colors of the sunset still lingered, casting a faint glow on the edges of the rooftop.

Without saying a word, she made her way upstairs to the terrace, her quiet refuge from the chaos below. The evening air was cooler now, wrapping her in a soft embrace as she stood by the railing. She fixed her gaze on the horizon, the last rays of the sun slipping away, leaving a cascade of pinks and oranges in their wake.

With every passing moment, her heart clung to a flicker of hope. "Maybe now," she thought. "Maybe Buddy will show up."

The minutes stretched on, but the terrace remained silent, save for the gentle whispers of the wind. Lilly closed her eyes tightly, willing away the ache that had settled in her chest. She wished desperately for Buddy to appear, to break through the stillness and reassure her that she wasn't as alone as she felt.

But the day ended without a sign of him.

As darkness enveloped the world, Lilly sighed, leaning her head against the cool metal of the railing. Her hands gripped it tightly as if anchoring herself against the tide of emotions threatening to overwhelm her.

Finally, she whispered softly to the night sky, "Maybe tomorrow."

She lingered there for a few more moments, the silence now her only companion, before descending the stairs. With a heavy heart, she prepared for bed, carrying the hope of a brighter tomorrow into her dreams.

It's been many days since buddy showed up in her life. Her days went by in a monotonous blur. She went to school, attended her classes, but her mind often drifted, her body feeling heavier than ever. It was as if her connection with Buddy, however fleeting, had given her a sense of stability. Without him, she felt empty again—like a piece of herself was missing.

She kept herself busy, trying to push away the dark thoughts that tried to creep back in. Her parents noticed her distance, but they didn't ask her about it. They never did.

But despite her efforts to keep going, Lilly couldn't escape the feelings that had haunted her for years. The weight of her past, the anxiety that lurked just beneath the surface, was always there, waiting to resurface.

Then, one afternoon, as she was walking home from school, she was suddenly jolted from her thoughts.

Out of nowhere, a man grabbed her arm from behind, pulling her toward a dark alley. Her heart pounded in her chest, the old familiar feeling of helplessness flooding her mind. The same fear, the same confusion, the same panic she had felt years ago. The moment felt like it was happening all over again—the shadows closing in, the threat of violence, the feeling that nobody would be able to save her.

But this time, something was different.

Screams rang out from nearby, people shouting, "Hey, leave her alone!" A couple of pedestrians, a man and a woman, rushed to her aid, pulling the man off her. Others gathered, and within moments, Lilly was surrounded by people who were helping her. The man who had grabbed her was restrained, held down by several people until the authorities arrived.

Lilly stood there, trembling, her breath coming in ragged gasps. She felt herself slipping, her hands clammy and shaking. Despite the fact that she had been saved, her mind couldn't process what had just happened. It was like a replay of her worst nightmare, only this time, the nightmare didn't end with her being taken. But in her head, it still felt like the same nightmare.

Her legs gave way beneath her, and she collapsed to the ground. The crowd was talking around her, but it sounded distant, muffled, like she was hearing it underwater. She tried to focus, tried to push through the dizziness, but her body refused to cooperate. Her hands trembled violently, and her chest tightened as if she couldn't get enough air.

The police arrived and asked her questions, but Lilly couldn't respond. Her mind was too clouded with panic and anxiety to form coherent thoughts. She just stared blankly ahead, her heart racing, feeling like she was suffocating in the middle of the chaos.

It wasn't just the fear of being grabbed—it was everything. The feelings of powerlessness, the lack of control, the old trauma that had never truly healed. It all came crashing back at once, and Lilly couldn't find her footing. It was as if her body and mind were still stuck in the past, trapped in that moment of terror. The crowd around her, the people trying to help, couldn't save her from what was happening inside her.

The authorities were called, and she was escorted to a nearby station for questioning. But even as she sat there, trying to pull herself together, Lilly couldn't shake the overwhelming sense of dread that clung to her.

Her mind kept replaying the moment—the man's hands on her, the fear, the helplessness. She could still feel the cold grip of his fingers as if it were happening all over again. It was as if the trauma had never left her, only lying dormant, waiting for the right moment to break free.

Despite the fact that she was physically okay, Lilly's anxiety only grew worse over the next few hours. She couldn't sleep that night. Her body felt like it was on high alert, every sound amplified, every movement making her jump. She could feel her pulse racing in her ears, and her hands were still shaking. Every time she closed her eyes, she saw the man's face, heard the sounds of the crowd, and felt the suffocating pressure that had gripped her.

Her parents didn't understand. They were relieved that she was safe, but they didn't know how deeply the incident had affected her. They didn't know how it had reopened the wounds she thought were healed. They didn't know that the trauma was still with her, always lurking just beneath the surface, waiting to erupt.

The next day at school, she tried to act normal, but the weight of what had happened was too much. Her classmates noticed her unease, but no one asked her about it. She felt the cold distance between her and the world, as if no one truly understood the war she was fighting in her own head. She walked through the halls like a ghost, detached from the reality around her.

Everyday moments—like sitting in class or walking through the crowded halls—felt like they were closing in on her. She couldn't breathe without feeling the tight grip of panic threatening to consume her. She kept thinking back to the moment when she had been grabbed, wishing she could erase it from her memory. But no matter how hard she tried to push the fear away, it stayed with her.

Back at home, Lilly retreated further into herself. Her parents didn't know how to help, and she didn't know how to explain it. Her panic attacks became more frequent, her anxiety worse than ever. The numbness she had once felt was replaced by an overwhelming flood of emotions that she couldn't control. She felt trapped, unable to escape the overwhelming weight of the trauma she was carrying.

She started avoiding places where she felt vulnerable—crowded areas, the park where she had been attacked. Every time she walked past the spot where the incident had happened, her body would tense, her heart racing. It was as if she was walking through a constant state of fear.

Lilly's world grew quieter – not in the literal sense but within herself. She began to withdraw from everything and everyone around her. Words became heavy, too heavy to speak. She stopped engaging in conversations at school, merely nodding when spoken to and avoiding eye contact. Her once timid attempts to blend in faded entirely as she sank into a silence that seemed unbreakable.

At home, the chaos was ever-present. Her parents' arguments filled the house, a constant reminder of the disarray she couldn't escape. Instead of confronting it, Lilly chose avoidance. She returned from school each day, her shoulders slumped, her face blank, and retreated to the only place where she could find a semblance of peace: the terrace. There, she watched the sunset in solitude, the fading colors of the sky her only solace.

As the sun disappeared beyond the horizon, she would close her eyes and imagine herself dissolving into the stillness, far away from the noise. This daily ritual became her anchor, though it provided little comfort.

At night, she sought escape through music. Plugging in her headphones, she turned the volume high, drowning out the shouts and arguments from downstairs. The music filled the emptiness, a sound barrier against the chaos. She would fall asleep with the songs playing, hoping they would keep the nightmares and the memories at bay.

But even in sleep, there was no reprieve. Lilly was trapped in a cycle of going through the motions, existing but not truly living. The isolation became her armor, protecting her from further hurt but also locking her deeper within herself.

One evening, as Lilly sat on the terrace watching the sunset, lost in her usual quiet, she heard a familiar voice call her name from behind.

"Lilly," the voice said softly, almost hesitantly.

She turned, her heart skipping a beat, and there he was—Buddy. He stood at the entrance to the terrace, his usual calm demeanor radiating a quiet confidence.

"Where have you been?" Lilly blurted out before she could stop herself. But Buddy only smiled faintly, not answering her question.

He walked toward her and stopped just a few feet away. Looking out at the sky, he took a deep breath, his chest rising and falling as if he were savoring the moment. Then, without a word, he stepped closer and stood beside her, their shoulders almost touching, both watching the sunset in silence.

For a moment, neither of them spoke. The hues of orange, pink, and purple painted the sky, casting a serene glow over the scene. The silence wasn't awkward but instead carried a comforting weight, like an unspoken understanding between two kindred souls.

"You missed the sunsets," Lilly finally said, her voice barely above a whisper.

Buddy turned his head slightly toward her and replied with a small smile, "I didn't miss them; I was waiting for the right one."

Lilly looked at him, confused but unwilling to press further. It was the first time in days that the terrace didn't feel so lonely.

As the sky darkened and the colors of the sunset faded into twilight, Lilly broke the silence. Her voice trembled slightly, the weight of her thoughts pressing heavily on her chest.

"Buddy," she began hesitantly, her eyes fixed on the horizon, "what is the meaning of life?"

Her question hung in the air, delicate and fragile, like the last rays of sunlight. Buddy didn't answer immediately. Instead, he inhaled deeply, his gaze unwavering as he stared into the distance.

After a moment, he smiled—a soft, understanding smile that made it seem as though he carried the wisdom of countless lifetimes.

"The meaning of life," he said, his voice calm yet profound, "is not a single answer, Lilly. It's a journey, a collection of moments, choices, and lessons. It's about finding purpose in the chaos, growth in the pain, and beauty in the fleeting."

Lilly glanced at him, her expression a mixture of curiosity and confusion.

"But what if it's too hard? What if it's just pain, day after day?" she asked, her voice barely above a whisper.

Buddy's smile didn't waver. "Pain is a teacher, Lilly, not a punishment. Every scar, every tear—it shapes who you are. Life isn't about avoiding the storms; it's about learning how to dance in the rain. You're stronger than you think, even when you don't feel it."

Lilly looked back at the darkening sky, her mind wrestling with his words. She didn't fully understand them yet, but they planted a small seed of hope—a quiet promise that, perhaps, life could hold meaning even in its darkest moments.

Buddy's presence felt steady, grounding, as if he were an anchor keeping her from drifting too far into despair.

As the night deepened, Lilly's thoughts spiraled further. She turned to Buddy, her eyes filled with the weight of unspoken questions.

"Buddy," she asked softly, "is there really a purpose for being alive? Or is it just something people say to keep going?"

Buddy didn't respond immediately. He tilted his head slightly, as if carefully choosing his words. The faint breeze ruffled his hair as he let out a thoughtful sigh.

"Purpose, Lilly, isn't something that's handed to us," he began, his voice steady and soothing. "It's something we create. Some people find it in their passions, others in the people they love, and sometimes, it's in the small acts we do without even realizing it—like the way you watch the sunset every evening. That's a purpose too, to seek peace in the chaos."

Lilly frowned, her voice tinged with skepticism. "But what if I can't find it? What if I never do?"

Buddy looked at her, his gaze warm and filled with quiet reassurance. "Even then, the journey of searching for it is worth living for. Life isn't just about the destination—it's about every step you take along the way. Sometimes, Lilly, just staying alive, enduring the hard days, and hoping for better ones... that's purpose enough. And who knows, maybe you'll stumble upon it when you least expect it."

Lilly's expression softened. She didn't have the energy to argue, and maybe, just maybe, Buddy's words held a truth she hadn't yet considered.

Lilly's mind was restless, her questions flowing like an endless tide. She turned to Buddy once more, her voice trembling, yet filled with a deep yearning for understanding.

"Buddy," she asked, "why is there good and why is there bad? And why... why is it that all I ever see are bad people?"

Buddy's response came swiftly, as though he had anticipated this question all along.

"Good and bad, Lilly," he began, his tone calm yet profound, "are like light and shadow. They're two sides of the same coin, and one cannot exist without the other. If everything were good, we wouldn't recognize its value; it would lose its meaning. The bad moments, as cruel as they seem, are what teach us to appreciate the good when it comes."

Lilly frowned, her lips quivering. "But why does it feel like the bad outweighs the good? Why does it feel like people... like they only bring pain?"

Buddy's eyes softened, a glimmer of understanding in his gaze. "That's because pain leaves deeper marks than joy, Lilly. It lingers, makes itself known, and demands to be felt. Goodness, on the other hand, often comes quietly – it doesn't shout or force itself upon you. It's like a whisper in the chaos, and sometimes, it takes effort to notice it."

He paused for a moment, his gaze fixed on the distant horizon. "But just because bad people seem louder doesn't mean good people don't exist. They do. Maybe they're quieter, or maybe they're too far away for you to see them right now. But trust me, Lilly, the world has both. And so do you. You have the choice to be a light for others or to let the shadows consume you."

Lilly stared at him, her emotions a tangle of confusion and clarity. Buddy's words were simple, yet they felt heavy with meaning.

"Do you think I can be that light?" she asked hesitantly.

Buddy smiled faintly, his voice kind but firm. "I know you can. Because even in your darkest moments, you've been looking for hope. That, Lilly, is what makes you stronger than you think."

For a moment, Lilly let his words sink in. She still wasn't sure she believed them, but deep down, a small flicker of hope began to stir

Lilly's voice trembled as she poured out her pain, her words carrying the weight of years of silence and yet she asked.

"The moment I try to speak, they shut me out with their laughs," she said, her tone bitter and broken. "The moment I try to be brave, they show me what fear looks like. The moment I ask for a bond with my family, they push me away, lost in their own egos. Buddy... when the whole universe tells me I don't belong here, what's the point of living?"

Buddy turned to her, his gaze steady but full of compassion. He didn't speak immediately, as if he were carefully choosing the words she needed to hear most. Finally, he exhaled deeply and answered.

"Lilly," he said softly, "the universe doesn't decide whether you belong. You do. The people around you, the situations you face—they don't define your worth or your place in this world. They only reflect their own chaos, their own fears and flaws. What you're feeling isn't a verdict from the universe; it's the weight of other people's shadows pressing against your light."

He paused, letting his words settle before continuing. "The point of living, Lilly, isn't to convince the world you belong. It's to find the things that make you feel alive. It's to create meaning, even if it's just for yourself. Those laughs, those fears, that distance—they don't have to be the final word. You have a voice, a strength, and a heart that's still beating. That's reason enough to keep going."

Lilly's eyes welled up, and she bit her lip, trying to hold back the flood of emotions. "But... it feels so lonely. Like there's no one who truly understands."

Buddy's expression softened further. "Loneliness is hard, I know," he admitted. "But sometimes, it's in the quiet spaces of loneliness that you discover yourself. You've already survived so much, Lilly. You've fought battles others can't see. That strength, that resilience—that's where you belong. Not in the approval of those who laugh or ignore, but in the space you carve out for yourself, where you can breathe freely and grow."

Lilly wiped her eyes, still unsure, but Buddy's words wrapped around her like a fragile cocoon. She didn't know if she could believe everything he said yet

Lilly's voice wavered as she hesitated before asking her next question. Her gaze was fixed on the fading hues of the sunset, but her mind was swirling with uncertainty.

"When I wished for a friend the first time, I got Kathey," she began, her voice barely a whisper. "And now, I wished again, and you came, Buddy. But what if... what if you also leave me? What if you leave me in the middle of chaos, throwing me into even more confusion?"

Buddy turned toward her, his expression unreadable at first. He didn't rush to respond, letting her words hang in the air like a fragile thread. After a long pause, he finally spoke, his tone steady but gentle.

"Lilly," he said, "friends, real or imagined, don't leave you empty-handed. Kathey may not be here anymore, but didn't she leave you with something? A feeling of being understood, a glimpse of what it's like to be seen without judgment? Even in her absence, those memories shaped you, gave you strength, and taught you what it means to connect."

He shifted his gaze to the horizon, as though searching for the right words. "As for me," he continued, "whether I stay or go isn't what matters most. What matters is what I leave behind if I have to go. My purpose isn't to take away your pain but to help you see that you can handle it, that you can find your own way out of the chaos. If one day I'm no longer here, you'll still have everything we've shared—the conversations, the moments of clarity, the hope. Those don't vanish when a friend does."

Lilly's hands gripped the edge of the terrace railing tightly, her knuckles turning white. "But what if I'm not strong enough to carry it alone?"

Buddy smiled softly, an almost bittersweet expression. "You're stronger than you think, Lilly. You've already carried so much more than anyone should have to. You're here, asking these questions, fighting to understand and survive. That's not weakness—it's courage. And if I ever have to leave, it won't be to throw you into confusion. It'll be because you're ready to walk the next part of your journey on your own, whether you realize it or not."

Lilly didn't respond to Buddy's words. Instead, she stood quietly for a moment, her eyes still fixed on the horizon where the last rays of sunlight disappeared. Without hesitation, she asked her next question, her tone calm yet probing.

"Buddy," she began, "why do elderly people act so insecure about their lives? And why is it that they don't listen to anything a child says, but they'll blindly believe another elder, even if it makes no sense?"

Buddy turned to her, a flicker of amusement softening his expression. He let out a small chuckle before speaking. "That's a sharp question, Lilly. But it's a valid one."

He leaned against the railing, his gaze thoughtful as he continued. "You see, with age comes experience, but also fear. When people grow older, they've lived through so many ups and downs that it leaves them constantly questioning what's next. That insecurity, as you put it, often stems from the awareness of how fragile life can be. The more you've seen, the more cautious you become."

Buddy paused, glancing at Lilly to ensure she was following. She nodded slightly, encouraging him to continue.

"As for why they don't listen to children," he said, "it's not because children aren't wise—far from it. Sometimes, children have insights that adults overlook. But elders tend to think their years of experience automatically make their perspective superior. They trust others their age because they assume shared experience equals understanding."

He straightened up, his voice softening. "It's not fair, I know. They forget that wisdom doesn't always come with age – it comes with understanding. And often, children see the world with a clarity that adults lose somewhere along the way. Their insecurity blinds them to that, making them cling to familiar voices instead of fresh ones."

Lilly frowned slightly, processing his words. "So they're scared?"

Buddy nodded. "In a way, yes. Fear of being wrong, fear of losing control, fear of their place in the world slipping away. It's not always intentional, but it can hurt others – especially someone like you, who's trying so hard to be heard."

Lilly didn't say anything, but her furrowed brow suggested she was turning his explanation over in her mind. Buddy let her have her silence, watching as the first stars began to dot the evening sky.

Lilly stayed quiet for a while, her eyes fixed on the stars now spreading across the night sky. Then, in a voice that wavered slightly, she asked, "Buddy, most people learn about fears, insecurities, and vulnerabilities when they're older, right? Like in their adulthood or maybe at the end of their teenage years. Then… why do I have to see all these things now? Why did it all come to me so early?"

Buddy turned to her, his gaze gentle yet steady. He took a deep breath, his tone soft but firm. "Lilly, life doesn't follow a fixed script for anyone. There's no rulebook that says pain or fear only come at a certain age. Some people face their struggles early, while others encounter them later. It's not about fairness – it's about timing."

Lilly's eyes glistened, but she didn't look at Buddy. Instead, she kept staring at the sky, waiting for him to continue.

"Think of it this way," Buddy said, his voice carrying a calm clarity. "The lessons life throws at us aren't about when they come—they're about what we do with them. You're seeing the world's shadows now, earlier than most, yes. But it also means you have a chance to grow stronger, wiser, and more understanding before many others even realize what's out there. You're learning to navigate the storm when others are still in calm waters."

Lilly clenched her fists slightly, her voice trembling. "But it's so hard, Buddy. Why couldn't I just... have a normal childhood? Why couldn't I just be like everyone else?"

Buddy placed a hand on the railing beside her, his expression pained but resolute. "I won't lie, Lilly—it's unfair. No one deserves to carry such heavy burdens, especially not at your age. But the fact that you're still standing, still asking questions, still searching for meaning—it shows how strong you are, even if you don't feel it."

He paused, glancing at her. "You're not broken, Lilly. You're growing. And while it hurts now, this pain is shaping you into someone who will one day see the world differently—not through fear or bitterness, but with a deeper understanding and compassion. You might not see it yet, but you're building something inside you that no one can take away."

Lilly finally looked at Buddy, her expression a mixture of anger, sadness, and something else—something close to hope. "But... it still hurts," she whispered.

"I know it does," Buddy said gently. "And it's okay to feel that hurt. Just remember, you're not alone in this—not anymore."

His words hung in the air like a comforting presence, as the stars twinkled above them, silently witnessing their conversation.

Lilly, with no hesitation, tilted her head slightly and asked, her voice laced with frustration, "Buddy, people always say life gives you what you need, not what you want. But why is my life not giving me what I need or what I want? Why does it feel like it's taking everything away instead?"

Buddy sighed softly, his gaze shifting to the horizon where the last remnants of sunlight lingered. After a moment of silence, he turned to her with an understanding expression.

"Lilly," he began, "people say that phrase because they believe life has a way of balancing itself—of providing lessons or opportunities that shape us, even if they're not what we think we need or desire. But the truth is, life is… unpredictable. It doesn't always work like a gift-giving machine, neatly handing over what you hope for or even what you think you need."

Lilly frowned, her shoulders slumping slightly. "Then what's the point, Buddy? If life doesn't care about what I want or need, why even bother?"

Buddy's voice softened, carrying a steady warmth. "Life doesn't hand us everything on a silver platter, Lilly, but it also doesn't leave us completely empty-handed. Sometimes, the things we need are hidden in places we'd never think to look—within struggles, in the smallest moments, or in the people we meet. And sometimes, it's up to us to go and find them."

Lilly remained silent, her expression heavy with doubt.

Buddy continued, his tone unwavering. "You feel like life isn't giving you anything right now, but think about this: the fact that you're sitting here, asking these questions, searching for meaning—it means you haven't given up. That's life giving you resilience, even if it feels invisible right now. And as for what you want… sometimes it takes time. Sometimes it's about creating space for the things you desire, even in the middle of the chaos."

"But Buddy," Lilly said, her voice cracking, "I don't know how to find those things. I don't even know what I'm looking for anymore."

Buddy smiled faintly, a mixture of sadness and hope. "You're looking for peace, for connection, for understanding. Those are hard to find, but not impossible. And Lilly, the first step isn't about waiting for life to hand them to you—it's about believing you deserve them."

Lilly looked at him, her expression a mix of skepticism and curiosity. "Do I really deserve them?"

"Yes," Buddy said firmly. "More than anything. And one day, you'll believe that too."

The words lingered in the air, settling into the quiet between them. Lilly didn't reply, but she didn't look away, either. Something about Buddy's presence—his unwavering certainty—made her feel, just for a moment, that maybe he was right.

Lilly's voice was barely above a whisper when she first asked, "Do they face any punishment for what they've done?" Her eyes drifted downward, as if the question had been too heavy for her to ask out loud. But then, with a sudden shift, she raised her gaze and asked again, this time more firmly, "Do people face punishment after they do bad things to others?"

Buddy paused, his expression thoughtful, as if the weight of the question had struck him as well. He took a deep breath, then answered, his voice calm but steady.

"Lilly, that's a tough question. The idea of punishment is something we often associate with justice—consequences for our actions. And in a perfect world, yes, people would face consequences for hurting others. It seems like the right thing to happen, right?" He looked at her, as if checking for her agreement.

Lilly nodded slightly, a look of frustration crossing her face. "Then why do some people just get away with it? Why does it feel like they never face the consequences of their actions?"

Buddy's eyes softened, his expression sympathetic. "I get it, Lilly. It's hard to understand why some people seem to escape without paying for the harm they've caused. But the truth is, punishment doesn't always come in the form we expect. It's not always immediate or obvious. Sometimes, the consequences of bad actions are invisible, like the pain they leave behind, or the way they change the way others see the world."

Lilly clenched her fists, her anger bubbling up. "But that's not fair! Why do they get to live their lives, while we carry the weight of their actions?"

Buddy sighed, his gaze fixed on the horizon. "I wish I could tell you that life always balances things out, but sometimes it doesn't. Sometimes, people live their lives without facing the consequences of what they've done. But that doesn't mean they're immune to the effects of their choices. The guilt, the regret, the fear of being found out—those are things that can haunt a person, even if they never show it."

Lilly was silent for a moment, her heart heavy with the injustice she felt. "So… no one really pays the price for hurting others?"

"Not always in the way we expect," Buddy replied gently. "But don't mistake that for saying they don't pay at all. The consequences of their actions may not always be visible to the outside world, but they still have to live with them. And sometimes, the hardest punishment is the one we give ourselves—the regret, the guilt, the knowledge of what we've done."

Lilly's eyes shifted, a quiet understanding beginning to form behind her frustration. "So... even if they don't get punished, they still have to live with the consequences?"

Buddy nodded slowly. "Yes. It may not always seem fair, but in the end, everyone carries the weight of their choices in some way, even if it's invisible to the rest of the world."

As the night stretched on, with the deep silence of midnight surrounding them, Lilly found herself standing still, her gaze lost in the vastness of the dark sky. The world felt distant, the weight of the past pressing down on her as the quiet seemed to amplify her thoughts.

For the first time in what felt like forever, she turned to Buddy, her voice barely a whisper, carried away by the gentle breeze that swept across the terrace.

"Buddy... For the actions of others, Kathey had to go through all that pain. And she gave up. The girl who was once the source of my strength, my hope—now she's gone. Without her... how am I supposed to make it? How do I keep going without her?"

The words hung in the air, heavy and vulnerable, swallowed by the stillness of the night. As the midnight hour loomed, Lilly felt the sharp sting of her loss, the absence of the one person who had understood her, the one who had shared in her silent suffering.

Buddy stood there for a moment, his gaze shifting toward the stars as if contemplating her question, the midnight air around them heavy with silence. Finally, he turned to Lilly, his voice calm, yet laced with a sense of understanding that only he could offer.

"You know, Lilly," he began, his words soft but full of weight, "Sometimes the people who give us strength are also the ones who teach us the hardest lessons. Kathey was your strength, yes, but she was also a reminder that we can't carry each other forever. We all have our battles, and sometimes, we have to fight them alone. But that doesn't mean you've lost the lessons she gave you."

He paused, letting the quiet settle around them before continuing. "You've already been through so much. You've already learned how to survive, how to rise up after every fall. And that strength... it's still inside you, even if you can't feel it right now. You're not starting from scratch, Lilly. You're starting from a place where you've already proven you can keep going, even when everything feels impossible."

Buddy gave a small, reassuring smile. "You're not alone, not really. You carry her with you—her strength, her love, and her belief in you. And maybe that's all you need to keep moving forward. Trust that you'll find new sources of strength, new friends, and that you'll continue to grow from everything you've faced."

With those words, the midnight air felt a little lighter, as if the weight of Lilly's heart had lifted just enough for her to breathe again.

As the night stretched on, Lilly remained perched on the terrace, her mind still racing with the questions that Buddy had answered and those that lingered unanswered. The stars twinkled softly above, but there was an emptiness in the air—a silence that seemed to echo louder than any words. The clock ticked away, and yet, there was no sign of her parents. They hadn't called. They hadn't even bothered to check in. The absence of their presence, the absence of their care, felt like a heavy weight pressing against her chest.

Her thoughts kept circling back to everything Buddy had said, and yet, there was still a part of her, a small corner of her heart, that wondered if any of it truly mattered. After all, if her own parents couldn't even care enough to be home or make sure she was okay, how could anyone else? Was there really hope for connection, for love, or was everything always destined to fade into emptiness?

The sky slowly began to shift. The stars, once so vibrant in the deep night, now began to dim as the first rays of dawn crept into the horizon. A faint light appeared at the edge of the sky, chasing away the darkness, yet it didn't bring with it the sense of relief Lilly had hoped for. The brightness felt cold, distant, like an unfamiliar presence she didn't know how to trust.

As the first light of morning began to paint the sky in shades of pale blue, Lilly remained on the terrace, her heart heavy with questions, her mind lost in the turmoil of her emotions. The night had moved forward, but it had left behind more questions than answers. And as the day began, Lilly wasn't sure if she was ready to face whatever it might bring.

Lilly's questions didn't stop; they flowed out of her, one after another, each more desperate than the last. With each passing moment, she sought understanding, something to hold onto, something that would make sense of everything that had happened—the pain, the confusion, the loneliness. Buddy stood beside her, as unwavering as ever, answering each question with a calmness that felt almost unnatural.

"Why does the world feel so empty sometimes, Buddy? Why do people seem so distant, even when they're close?"

Buddy took a deep breath, his eyes fixed on the horizon where the first light of the sun began to appear, stretching its warmth over the land. "The world feels empty because we're often looking for something to fill us from the outside, Lilly. But the real answers, the real peace, come from within. People seem distant because they haven't learned to connect with themselves. They can't connect with others if they don't understand themselves first."

Lilly's gaze shifted to the ground, her mind swirling. "But why does it have to be this way? Why do we have to learn everything the hard way? Why do I have to go through all this pain?"

Buddy's voice softened, almost like a whisper against the wind. "Pain is not the enemy, Lilly. It's the teacher. It shows you your strength, your vulnerability, and your capacity for growth. Life isn't about avoiding pain; it's about learning how to carry it and still move forward."

Lilly swallowed hard, feeling the weight of his words pressing on her chest. The sun had risen higher now, the warmth slowly spreading across the sky, but inside, Lilly still felt cold. "But sometimes, I don't think I have the strength. I've already lost so much. And I feel like I keep losing more."

Buddy's gaze softened, his expression sincere. "You haven't lost anything, Lilly. Everything you've been through, every loss, every heartache—it's all a part of your journey. You don't lose yourself through pain. You find yourself."

Lilly let out a long sigh, the weight of the world still heavy on her shoulders. "What if I'm too far gone? What if I can't find my way back?"

Buddy stepped closer, placing a hand on her shoulder. "You're not too far gone, Lilly. No one is. You just have to be willing to face the darkness to find the light. It's all there, inside you. You've always had it. You just need to believe it."

As the sun rose higher in the sky, casting its golden glow on everything around them, Lilly felt something shift within her. It wasn't a sudden rush of clarity or understanding, but something subtle. A flicker of hope. A whisper that maybe, just maybe, she wasn't as lost as she had believed.

The sun was high now, and with its rise, Lilly realized that the answers might not come all at once, that the questions might never fully stop—but with each one, she was finding herself a little more, and that, perhaps, was the most important thing of all.

But as she spoke, she didn't hear the footsteps approaching from behind—the soft tap of shoes on the stairs, the creak of the door opening. Her mother had come home.

Lilly's mother had been frantic when she couldn't find her daughter inside the house. She searched the rooms, the kitchen, the living room. No sign of Lilly, no sign of her husband either. Panic rose in her chest as she hurried up the stairs to the terrace. It was there, on the quiet, sunlit terrace, that she found Lilly.

Lilly was sitting cross-legged, her face turned towards the sky, speaking to someone. Her hands moved as though she were emphasizing a point, and her voice was calm, soft—almost as if she was sharing a secret with a dear friend.

Her mother froze at the sight. She could hear Lilly speaking, but no one else was there.

"Lilly..." Her voice broke through the quiet. "Who are you talking to, sweetie?"

Lilly's head turned slightly, and she smiled softly, almost as if she were sharing a special moment with someone only she could see. "Mom, this is Buddy. My best friend."

The words hit her mother like a cold wave. She blinked, searching the space around Lilly. There was no one else. The terrace was empty.

Her heart began to race as she took a step closer. "Buddy?" she repeated, trying to steady her voice. "Lilly, there's no one here. Who are you really talking to?"

Lilly looked at her mother, her smile fading slightly. "But... Buddy's right here," she said, her voice tinged with confusion. "He's my friend. He's always here when I need him."

Her mother's breath caught in her throat. A cold chill ran down her spine. She had heard of things like this—delusions, hallucinations—but she never thought it could happen to her child. She glanced around again, her mind spinning, but there was no one there.

Without thinking, her hands trembled as she pulled out her phone and quickly dialed her husband. Her voice shook as she explained the situation. "She's talking to someone… But there's no one there, David. She's talking to herself. She's saying his name is Buddy."

Lilly's mother felt a deep sense of panic, her mind racing with questions. What was happening to her daughter? Was it the stress? Was it something more? She stood frozen for a moment, watching her daughter talk to the empty space beside her, her heart sinking.

She tried to call lilly's father to explain him about lilly's situation. But he wasn't picking the call, lilly's mother tried to call him again and again, she could barely hold herself together. She gave up calling him after many dials. Her eyes turned back to lilly, who has still smiling softly, engaged in her conversation.

"Lilly, sweetheart," she said, trying to keep her voice gentle, though her words trembled. "Come inside, please. We need to talk."

But Lilly didn't respond right away. She just sat there, her gaze still locked on the empty space beside her.

"Lilly, honey, please..." Her mother's voice broke as she approached her daughter.

Lilly slowly stood up, her gaze still fixed on the space Buddy would have occupied. She turned to face her mother, a confused, childlike innocence in her eyes. "I don't want to go inside, Mom. Buddy's still here. He's waiting."

But her mother, overwhelmed with fear and uncertainty, couldn't process the words. The image of her daughter speaking to an invisible friend—the look on her face, the way she acted so sure of Buddy's presence—made her heart ache with confusion and worry.

"Lilly, we need to get some help," she whispered, taking Lilly's hand and leading her back toward the door. But in her heart, she feared what this might mean for her daughter's future.

As Lilly's mother panicked, she immediately contacted a psychiatrist. Her voice shaky as she explained the situation over the phone, telling them about Lilly's apparent imaginary friend, Buddy, and her concerning behavior. The psychiatrist agreed to see them as soon as possible, but there was no sign of Lilly's father. He couldn't make it in time due to work, leaving Lilly's mother to take charge alone.

She tried to stay calm, but worry and fear tugged at her heart as she led Lilly to the car. Lilly, unaware of the gravity of the situation, walked beside her mother with a peaceful expression on her face. She still seemed to be in her world, speaking occasionally to Buddy, who only Lilly could see.

The ride to the psychiatrist's office felt long, and with each passing minute, Lilly's mother felt a heavy weight of doubt and fear pressing on her chest. She wanted to believe that everything would be okay, but deep down, a terrifying thought nagged at her—What if Buddy wasn't just a figment of Lilly's imagination? What if there was something more, something beyond her understanding?

As they arrived at the psychiatrist's office, Lilly didn't protest. She didn't resist when her mother gently ushered her inside. The receptionist led them to a small, quiet room where Lilly would meet with the psychiatrist.

The psychiatrist, an older man with a calm demeanor, greeted them and introduced himself. Lilly's mother, barely able to contain her emotions, explained everything—how Lilly had been speaking to an invisible friend for days, how she hadn't been acting like herself, and how concerned she was for her daughter's well-being.

The psychiatrist nodded, listening carefully, and then turned his attention to Lilly. He asked her a few questions about Buddy and the conversations they had. Lilly, however, didn't seem distressed. She spoke about Buddy with an innocent affection, telling the psychiatrist how Buddy was always there to answer her questions, how he made her feel less alone.

After some time, the psychiatrist decided that it was best to begin with a hypnosis session. He explained that it would help Lilly explore her thoughts and emotions in a relaxed state, where she could communicate more freely.

Lilly's mother watched anxiously from a chair in the corner as the psychiatrist slowly guided Lilly into a deep trance. As Lilly's eyes fluttered closed and her body relaxed, the psychiatrist began to ask questions.

"Lilly," he said gently, "I want you to tell me about Buddy. Who is Buddy, and why is he so important to you?"

In the trance-like state, Lilly responded calmly, "Buddy is my best friend. He listens to me, and he answers all my questions. He helps me when I feel sad or confused."

The psychiatrist nodded and then asked, "Lilly, do you know if Buddy is real or if he's someone you created?"

Lilly's face remained calm, but she shook her head slightly. "No. Buddy is real. He's not just in my head. He's here with me. He talks to me, and I talk to him. He's not imaginary. He's my friend."

The psychiatrist paused, a flicker of concern crossing his face. He looked at Lilly's mother, who was now visibly trembling. She had hoped that this would be just a phase, that Lilly would see through it eventually. But it was clear from Lilly's words that she truly believed Buddy was real.

The psychiatrist gently guided Lilly back from the trance. As she opened her eyes, she seemed peaceful, but there was no change in her belief. Buddy was still real to her. The psychiatrist explained to Lilly's mother that what they were dealing with was likely a deep emotional struggle for Lilly, one that had manifested through her belief in Buddy. He was more than an imaginary friend—he was a coping mechanism, a way for Lilly to deal with the overwhelming emotions and loneliness she felt.

But Lilly wasn't ready to accept that. She refused to believe that Buddy wasn't real. She wasn't ready to face the pain of realizing that her only source of comfort, the one person who truly understood her, was nothing more than a projection of her own mind.

The psychiatrist prescribed medication to help manage Lilly's symptoms and suggested therapy to help her deal with her past trauma and begin healing. But the most important thing, he said, would be addressing the emotional disconnect between Lilly and her family. They needed to communicate better, understand each other more, and start healing together.

As Lilly's mother led her back home, her heart was heavy. The road ahead would be long. The psychiatrist's words echoed in her mind—Buddy wasn't real, but to Lilly, he was. And as much as she wanted to help Lilly understand, she also feared what might happen if Lilly couldn't face the truth.

When they returned home, Lilly's mother couldn't help but feel a deep sadness for her daughter. Buddy might not be real, but Lilly's attachment to him was as real as any other relationship. Would Lilly ever be able to see past this creation? Or would Buddy forever be her only friend, the one constant in a world that had never shown her much kindness?

Lilly's mother didn't have the answers. All she could do was try to be there for her, to guide her through the pain and the confusion. But it was clear that the journey ahead wouldn't be easy, and the healing process would take time.

When Lilly's father arrived home, he could sense the tension in the air immediately. The house was quieter than usual, and his wife's face was tense, her brows furrowed in a mix of frustration and concern. He placed his briefcase down by the door and looked at her, confused.

"What's going on?" he asked, his voice laced with concern. "You look like you've been through something."

Lilly's mother, unable to contain herself, started speaking, her voice rising in frustration. "You weren't here! I was dealing with Lilly, and she's not listening to anything! She's talking to herself, claiming someone named Buddy is real, and I had to take her to a psychiatrist without you even being here! You weren't here when I needed you. I had to do everything alone!"

Lilly's father took a moment, absorbing her words. He knew something had been off with Lilly for a while, but hearing it like this stung. He'd been so caught up with work that he hadn't realized how much his absence was affecting everything at home. But he didn't want to escalate things. He took a deep breath and looked at his wife with calm eyes.

"Listen," he said softly, his tone firm but gentle. "I know I've been absent, and I'm not excusing it. But I'm here now. I'm trying to help, but yelling won't fix anything. We need to stay calm and figure out the next steps for Lilly, not just argue about it."

Lilly's mother, still agitated, shook her head. "How can you be calm about this? She's talking to someone who doesn't exist! She's losing touch with reality, and we're just supposed to stay calm? You weren't here when I needed you the most."

Her voice broke, and tears started to well in her eyes. She felt the weight of it all – the sleepless nights, the worry about Lilly, the constant emotional burden. "I can't do this alone. I need you here."

Lilly's father stepped forward, his expression softening. "I know, and I'm sorry for not being here sooner. But I'm here now, and we need to be a team. I don't want to add to the chaos. We both want what's best for Lilly."

He reached out and gently placed his hand on her shoulder, trying to offer comfort. "Let's just take a step back, okay? We'll get through this together, but we can't help Lilly if we're both panicking."

Lilly's mother wiped her eyes, taking a deep breath. She nodded, her emotions still raw, but she knew her husband was right. They needed to come together for their daughter, not let the anger or frustration tear them apart.

Lilly's father added, "We'll figure out what's next. We need to keep calm and talk to Lilly. I'll help with whatever comes next, but let's take it one step at a time."

His voice had a steadiness to it that reminded Lilly's mother to pause and breathe. She wiped her face, feeling the tears slowly subside. She nodded slowly, still shaken but starting to feel a bit more grounded.

"I'll try," she murmured, feeling the weight of it all pressing on her chest.

Lilly's father gave her a reassuring nod. "We'll get through this. Together."

As the days passed, the tension in the household continued to rise. What had started as a moment of mutual understanding between Lilly's parents had slowly turned into a cycle of misunderstanding. The weight of their daughter's condition—the pills, the therapy, the endless concern—seemed to weigh on both of them in different ways, but neither knew how to break free from the growing divide between them.

Lilly's mother, still consumed by worry, found herself focusing on the practicalities—ensuring that Lilly took her medication, making sure the psychiatrist's appointments were scheduled, and keeping everything together on the surface. But her worry began to turn into frustration as she felt the emotional distance between her and Lilly growing. She didn't know how to reach her daughter anymore. She couldn't understand how Lilly could still hold on to her delusions about Buddy, and no matter how much she tried, it felt like her efforts were in vain.

Meanwhile, Lilly's father, though still trying to support the family, became more withdrawn. He had always been the calmer of the two, but his patience began to wear thin. He didn't know how to connect with Lilly, how to understand the depths of her pain. He kept telling himself that the therapy and the pills would eventually work, but deep down, he felt helpless. The emotional walls between him and his wife grew higher with each passing day.

One evening, as they sat in silence, Lilly's mother spoke up, her voice trembling with frustration. "She's not improving, we're doing everything we can, and yet nothing is changing. We've given her the pills, we've taken her to the therapist. What else is there? Why can't we help her?"

Lilly's father didn't respond right away. He stared at the floor, feeling the weight of his own guilt. "We're doing what we can," he said quietly. "But we're missing something... something important. It's not just the pills or the therapy. Lilly needs more than that. She needs us to be there. We can't just give her medicine and think that will fix everything. We need to be present, emotionally, but I... I don't know how."

His voice trailed off, and his wife's frustration turned to anger. "You don't know how? You've been distant for so long, and now you're telling me this? I'm trying my best, but you're just... you're not here, not really here! We're both just going through the motions, thinking that these pills will do all the work. But they won't! Lilly needs us, but she doesn't even know how to ask for it. And you—you're not even trying to understand her."

Her voice cracked with emotion as she continued, "I'm not even sure we're helping her anymore. All we're doing is adding to her confusion, her loneliness."

Lilly's father sighed, his frustration bubbling up. "I know you're doing your best, but yelling at me won't fix anything. I know you feel helpless, I feel it too, but we need to focus on how to be there for her, really be there—not just worry about the pills."

"That's easy for you to say," Lilly's mother snapped. "You're not the one who has to face her every day, who has to watch her fall apart."

The argument spiraled, and in the heat of it, both of them forgot to consider the one thing that Lilly needed most—attention and love. They had become so consumed by the routines, the constant worry, and their own frustrations that they lost sight of what was truly important. The medication was on schedule, the appointments were attended, but Lilly's emotional needs were neglected. They didn't notice the quiet pain in her eyes, the distance between them growing every day.

Lilly, for her part, had retreated even further into her silence. She still went to school, still took her medication, but at home, she became a shadow. She no longer sought comfort or attention from her parents. Instead, she spent hours in her room, staring at the walls or listening to music to drown out the sounds of her parents' arguments. Her connection with Buddy—her imaginary friend—was the only source of solace she had left, and even that was slipping away, as reality seemed to blur with her desires for something, anything, to fill the emptiness.

Each day, Lilly drifted further, and the gap between her and her parents widened. The love and attention they should have given her were buried beneath their own frustrations and misunderstandings. In their efforts to help her, they only made her feel more alone.

One day, as Lilly sat alone in her room, speaking softly to Buddy, she felt a strange calmness, as if everything in the world had slowed down. Buddy had been her constant companion, the one who answered her endless questions, the one who gave her hope when it felt like there was none left. For a moment, she thought she could hear his voice even though he hadn't spoken in days.

But suddenly, the door creaked open, and Lilly's mother walked in, holding the usual pill bottle in her hand. She passed right by Buddy without even noticing him, and continued towards Lilly with the medication.

Lilly froze, staring at her mother, the confusion building up inside her. Her mother didn't seem to see Buddy, didn't even acknowledge his presence. She simply walked up to Lilly and handed her the pills, the same routine they had followed for days, for weeks. Without thinking, Lilly opened her mouth, and her mother poured the water into it, just as she had done so many times before.

It wasn't until the water hit her throat that Lilly felt a wave of something sharp, something unsettling, sweep through her. Her eyes moved from the pills in her hand to the empty space beside her, where Buddy had been standing just moments ago. The realization hit her like a freight train, and the world seemed to tilt beneath her.

She could feel the weight of it—the truth she had been unwilling to face for so long.

Buddy wasn't real.

The tears began to well up in her eyes, and as they spilled down her cheeks, she couldn't stop them. She looked around the room, the absence of Buddy suddenly suffocating her. Her heart ached, and for the first time in a long while, she felt completely and utterly alone.

Lilly's mother didn't notice the change in her daughter, still focused on the task of making sure she took the pills. But Lilly's mind was racing, spiraling into the depths of the realization she had been avoiding for so long.

Buddy had been a figment of her imagination, a creation of her mind, born from her loneliness and desperation. But in that moment, as the last trace of his presence faded away, Lilly couldn't help but wonder: Had he ever really been there at all? Or had he been a ghost of her need for companionship, a fleeting illusion that now slipped away as quickly as it had arrived?

The silence that filled the room was deafening.

Lilly's mother, unaware of the storm that was unfolding inside her daughter, left the room, shutting the door quietly behind her. Lilly sat in the silence for what felt like hours, her heart heavy, the weight of her emotional isolation more unbearable than ever. She wiped her tears away, but it didn't matter. The truth had already settled in.

Buddy was gone.

After realizing that Buddy wasn't real, Lilly's mind was consumed by a storm of questions, doubts, and confusion. She couldn't understand how everything she had believed in had just vanished—like Buddy, like her sense of safety and control. Her emotions were a chaotic mix of grief, anger, and frustration, and she felt as though the walls around her were closing in. She needed space.

Her mind kept replaying all the events: her parents' fights, her inability to connect with anyone, and the overwhelming feeling of being trapped. The house—where she should have felt safe—felt like a cage. And with the loss of Buddy, it felt even more suffocating.

Lilly tried to block out the pain, but it only became louder. The uncertainty, the fear, and the sense of being completely alone overwhelmed her. She couldn't stay there any longer, not under the same roof, in the same house where everything felt broken. So, without a plan, without knowing where she was going, Lilly decided to leave.

She packed a small bag with a few essentials—nothing of real importance—just things to get by for a little while. She slipped out quietly, avoiding any confrontation or even a final goodbye. Her parents, as usual, were too caught up in their own arguments to notice.

Lilly stepped out of the house into the cold night air, feeling a mix of relief and fear. She didn't know where to go, but she needed to get away from everything. She just needed to escape, even if only for a short while, to clear her mind.

Time passed, and Lilly walked aimlessly around the streets, lost in her own thoughts. Meanwhile, at home, her parents remained oblivious to her absence until the usual medication time arrived. Her mother went to check on her, only to find the bed empty. Panic set in immediately.

She called out for Lilly, searching the house frantically, but there was no sign of her daughter.

Her father, still wrapped up in his own frustrations, was slow to react. But when he saw the genuine concern in his wife's face, he realized something was wrong. After several calls to neighbors and friends, and no sign of Lilly, the situation grew worse.

The realization hit them hard: Lilly was gone.

By evening, with no idea where Lilly had gone, her parents were forced to reach out for help. They made their way to the police station, a mix of guilt, fear, and confusion weighing heavily on them. They gave a detailed description of Lilly, her appearance, and the circumstances leading to her disappearance.

The officers reassured them that they would search for her, but the fear in their eyes was palpable. Her parents, once preoccupied with their own issues, were now fully aware that their daughter needed them—not just physically, but emotionally. They hadn't been there for Lilly in the ways that mattered, and now she was gone.

The police made a call for a search, and her parents sat in a quiet corner of the station, waiting, hoping for any news, but feeling powerless.

On the other hand, The cold wind brushed against Lilly's tear-streaked face as she kept running, her feet pounding against the pavement. She didn't know where she was headed; all she wanted was to escape. Escape from the house that never felt like home. Escape from the deafening arguments. Escape from her own thoughts, which now screamed louder than ever.

Her mind replayed the cruel whispers of doubt. "Buddy isn't real. He never was. Everything he said... it was all a lie." The voice echoed relentlessly, making her chest tighten as if the air itself was mocking her.

She rubbed her eyes with the back of her hands, wiping away tears, but they kept flowing. Her legs ached, her breath hitched, yet she didn't stop until—

Thud.

Her foot struck a jagged rock, and she stumbled forward, crashing onto the rough road. Pain shot up her knee, but it didn't matter. Lying there for a moment, Lilly let out a shaky breath and slowly pushed herself up, brushing dirt off her palms.

As she stood, her gaze lifted, and there it was—a large archway just ahead. The faded letters above it read: "New Horizons Orphanage."

Her chest tightened at the sight. Buddy. His voice, so vivid in her memory, replayed in her mind. "I'm just a boy from the streets, no parents... an orphan."

A fresh wave of tears threatened to spill, but she swallowed them back. Though her mind screamed that Buddy wasn't real, her heart clung to the faint hope of seeing him here. Maybe he was waiting for her inside. Maybe this was where she would find answers.

Shouldering her small bag, Lilly limped toward the gate and stepped inside. The soft laughter of children drifted through the air, mingling with the rustling of leaves. For a moment, the chaos in her mind quieted, replaced by a strange, unfamiliar stillness.

As Lilly stepped inside the orphanage gates, the hum of lively chatter and laughter contrasted sharply with the turmoil in her heart. She was greeted by a caretaker who noticed her tear-streaked face and weary appearance.

"Are you here to see someone, dear?" the caretaker asked gently.

Lilly hesitated, clutching the strap of her bag tightly. "No... I just... needed a place to be," she replied softly.

The caretaker studied her for a moment but decided not to press. "You're welcome to sit and rest. Take your time."

Lilly wandered further inside, observing the various people around her—children running about, a group of teenagers painting a mural on a wall, and a few adults tending to the garden. Despite the cheerful environment, a pang of sadness struck her heart.

As she sat on a bench, a little girl holding a frayed teddy bear approached her. "Hi! I'm Mia. What's your name?"

Lilly forced a small smile. "I'm Lilly."

Mia plopped down beside her, hugging her teddy tightly. "Are you sad? When I'm sad, I talk to Mr. Teddy. He always listens."

Lilly's eyes welled up again. "Sometimes... talking doesn't make it better," she murmured.

Mia tilted her head, puzzled. "But you're here now. Maybe someone can listen to you."

This simple exchange sparked something in Lilly. Over the next few hours, she began to interact with the residents of the orphanage, each sharing their stories of loss and resilience. It was a bittersweet experience for her—she found comfort in their courage but also felt her own vulnerabilities laid bare.

"Lilly," the caretaker said, her voice calm and measured. "I would like to ask that do you really have no one? No family, no home to go back to?"

Lilly felt her heart race. She gripped the strap of her bag tightly, her fingers trembling. "I told you," she replied softly, her gaze fixed on the ground. "I don't have anyone."

The caretaker crouched slightly to meet Lilly at eye level, her expression full of concern. "I know this isn't easy, sweetheart," she said. "But sometimes, we make decisions out of fear, not because they're what we truly need. Are you sure there's no one out there who would be worried about you?"

Lilly's throat tightened as a flood of memories threatened to overwhelm her: the endless shouting at home, the weight of her parents' indifference, and the crushing realization about Buddy. "I've been on my own for a long time," she murmured, the words feeling half-true and half-lie. "No one's looking for me. No one cares."

The caretaker studied her intently, noticing the pain hidden behind Lilly's quiet demeanor. "Alright," she said after a long pause. "I won't push you. But if you ever need to talk, I'm here. You're safe here, Lilly."

Lilly gave a small nod, her emotions swirling.

"Come on," the caretaker said, straightening up and gesturing toward the building. "Let me show you around and help you settle in."

The caretaker led Lilly through the quiet corridors of the orphanage, the sound of their footsteps echoing softly against the tiled floor. The building had an air of simplicity, with walls painted in pastel shades and small, framed artworks created by residents adorning the hallway.

Stopping at a door halfway down the corridor, the caretaker turned to Lilly with a gentle smile. "This will be your room," she said, pushing the door open.

Inside, the room was modest but cozy. Two single beds were placed on opposite sides, each neatly made with faded but clean sheets. A small wooden table sat between the beds, and a window let in soft, natural light that brightened the space.

"You'll be sharing this room with Mrs. Eleanor," the caretaker continued, gesturing to the bed nearest the window. "She's been with us for a few years now. A quiet soul, but I think you'll find her easy to talk to."

Lilly stepped inside cautiously, her eyes scanning the room. Sitting on the edge of the far bed was an older woman, her silver-streaked hair braided neatly over her shoulder. She looked up from the book in her hands and gave Lilly a warm, welcoming smile.

"Hello, dear," the woman said, her voice soft but steady. "what's your name."

Lilly nodded hesitantly and said "it's lilly", clutching the strap of her bag.

"Mrs. Eleanor," the caretaker said, addressing the older woman, "this is Lilly. She'll be sharing the room with you."

Eleanor's eyes softened as she observed Lilly's guarded posture. "It's lovely to meet you, Lilly. You can put your things wherever you like," she said, gesturing to the empty bed.

Lilly moved slowly to her side of the room, setting her bag down on the bed. The caretaker lingered by the door for a moment. "I'll leave you two to settle in," she said. "Dinner is at seven. If you need anything, Lilly, don't hesitate to find me."

With that, the caretaker left, leaving Lilly and Eleanor alone. For a moment, there was silence, save for the faint rustle of the wind outside the window.

Eleanor broke the quiet with a kind, measured tone. "It must have been a long day for you," she said, closing her book and setting it on the table. "Take your time settling in, dear. I'm here if you'd like to talk—or if you just need some quiet."

Lilly nodded, her defenses still firmly in place, but there was something comforting about Eleanor's calm demeanor. She sat on the edge of her bed, her thoughts swirling as she glanced out the window at the fading daylight.

A week had passed since Lilly arrived at New Horizons Orphanage, and life had begun to feel different. The first few days had been quiet for her—days of simply observing the lively environment. But slowly, she found herself being drawn into the warmth and rhythm of the place.

The orphanage was nothing like the chaotic house she had left behind. It was filled with voices—children laughing, teenagers debating about trivial things, and older residents sharing stories from their lives. Lilly found herself watching them from the sidelines at first, her heart aching but also curious.

By the third day, something shifted. One of the younger children, a boy no older than seven, tugged on her sleeve and asked her to help him draw a rainbow. Hesitant but unable to say no, she sat beside him with a pack of crayons. As they worked together, she felt a small spark of joy, something she hadn't experienced in what felt like ages.

Day by day, Lilly began to open up, even if just a little. A woman in her twenties invited her to join a game of cards with the older residents. A teenage girl asked for her opinion on how to braid her hair. Slowly, and without realizing it, Lilly started expressing herself—little things at first, like choosing a color for the game or giving an honest answer about the braid.

Eleanor, her roommate, watched these small changes unfold with quiet pride. She didn't push Lilly to talk about her past, but when Lilly needed a comforting presence, Eleanor was there.

One evening, as the sun dipped low in the sky, casting golden hues over the orphanage courtyard, Lilly sat with a group of children. They were playing a game, and Lilly found herself laughing—genuinely laughing—for the first time in years.

The weight of her past didn't disappear entirely, but it felt distant, muffled by the joy and love surrounding her. She no longer scanned every corner, expecting to see Buddy. The thought of him grew faint, tucked away in the recesses of her mind.

Days turned into moments where Lilly began to understand the beauty of sharing space with others, of feeling connected. She still avoided looking too closely at her own reflections in the mirror of life, but something within her was shifting. For the first time in a long time, she felt like maybe, just maybe, she belonged.

One night, as Lilly drifted into a restless sleep, her mind revisited the terrace with Buddy. The vivid image of Buddy standing beside her, offering comforting words, suddenly shifted. In the dream, Buddy, while mid-conversation, lost his footing and tumbled backward off the edge of the building. His last words echoed in Lilly's mind, "Lilly… no! Don't forget me…"

Lilly screamed in her sleep, jolting awake, her heart pounding in her chest. Her breath came in sharp gasps as the image of Buddy falling off the terrace lingered.

Across the room, Eleanor, the woman Lilly shared the room with, had woken up to Lilly's scream. Concerned, Eleanor quickly got up and went to her. She softly touched Lilly's shoulder, "Nightmare?"

Lilly nodded, her eyes wide with the lingering fear of the dream. Eleanor's voice was gentle as she reached for a glass of water from the table and handed it to Lilly.

As Lilly took the water, her hands trembling slightly, she took a few deep breaths, trying to calm herself. The nightmare still gripped her heart. She looked down at the glass in her hands, as if it could somehow hold all the emotions she hadn't processed in years.

"It felt so real," Lilly whispered, her voice shaky.

Eleanor sat down beside her. "I understand. Sometimes our minds bring us back to things we can't control. But you're here, Lilly. Safe."

Lilly let the words sink in, her throat tight. She realized she was no longer running from her emotions. "I don't want to forget, Eleanor," she confessed softly. "But I don't know how to stop feeling like I've lost everything."

Eleanor gently put her arm around Lilly, offering silent comfort. "Lilly, you haven't lost everything. You've lost pieces of yourself, yes, but you can rebuild them. Just like we rebuild ourselves every day here."

Lilly's mind wandered back to Buddy, to the terrace, to the feeling of abandonment and confusion. For the first time, she didn't feel angry at the idea of Buddy disappearing. She felt… tired. The endless search for something outside herself, for an answer that wasn't coming, had exhausted her.

After a few moments of silence, Lilly wiped her eyes and nodded slowly. "Maybe… maybe it's time to face everything, even if it hurts."

Eleanor smiled softly. "You're stronger than you think."

As the minutes passed and Lilly slowly started to regain her calm, Eleanor, sensing that Lilly needed more than just comfort, began to speak softly, her voice steady but filled with a quiet sorrow.

"You know," Eleanor began, staring out the window as if seeing a far-off memory, "I once had a family too. A husband… and two children." She paused, a fleeting sadness crossing her face.

Lilly, still holding the glass in her hands, listened attentively. Eleanor had always been kind to her, but Lilly hadn't known much about her past. She had assumed Eleanor's life had been easy—after all, she had a place to stay here, among the other people in the orphanage.

"My husband and I… we loved each other at one point. But life, it changes, doesn't it? People change. We drifted apart, and my children… they were caught in the middle. I tried, Lilly. I really did. But everything I did, nothing seemed to be enough for them. My husband left me, and the kids… they blamed me. They said I didn't love them enough. That I was too focused on myself, too lost in my own pain."

Eleanor's voice cracked for a moment, but she quickly regained her composure. She looked at Lilly, her eyes now more understanding. "The truth is, I didn't know how to love them properly. I was so caught up in my own hurt, in my own regrets, that I couldn't see what they needed. I failed them. And when they grew up, they left me. They told me I abandoned them when they needed me most. And I just... I couldn't make them understand."

Lilly was silent, processing the weight of Eleanor's words. She could see now how much pain Eleanor had carried with her all these years. And yet, despite the hurt, there was no bitterness in her voice—only a quiet longing, an aching desire to repair what had been broken.

"Now, they won't even speak to me," Eleanor continued, her voice soft and calm, as if the years of grief had turned her words into a gentle stream of truth. "They think I don't care, but I do. I always did. And if I could go back, if I could turn back time and show them how much I truly loved them... I would do it in a heartbeat. I would care for them the way they deserved. But that's not how life works, is it, Lilly?"

Lilly's eyes welled up with tears as she listened. For the first time, she felt a connection to someone who understood the heartache of loss and regret, even if it was a different kind of loss than her own. She had never really thought about how others could be caught in their own struggles, fighting battles that weren't so obvious from the outside.

"I'm sorry, Eleanor," Lilly whispered, her voice soft. "I didn't know. I didn't realize... that you were going through all of this too."

Eleanor smiled faintly, a tear slipping down her cheek. "Don't apologize, child. Sometimes we need to go through the darkest places to understand the light. And maybe that's what we're both doing right now."

As Eleanor finished her story, her voice soft and distant, Lilly sat still for a moment, letting the weight of her words settle inside her. She thought about her parents—their arguments, their distractions, the way they seemed unable to support her when she needed them most. It had always felt like they were lost in their own world, too consumed by their struggles to even notice hers. But now, as Eleanor spoke of her own battles with loss and regret, Lilly began to see things differently.

"I used to have nightmares too," Eleanor murmured, almost as if speaking to herself. "The hardest one was always the one where I'm far from my children, and I can never make things right. It haunts me, the thought that I could've done more for them. But the truth is... sometimes you can't change what's already been done. You can only move forward. It took me years to understand that."

Lilly blinked, her heart aching at the thought of Eleanor's pain. She realized that despite the distance and the coldness that had grown between them, Eleanor still loved her children deeply. The same way her parents loved her, even though they were struggling and couldn't understand what Lilly had been going through. They were not perfect, but they had their own battles—just like everyone else.

"I think... I think I understand now," Lilly whispered, her voice shaking slightly. "My parents... they were never there for me because they didn't know. They were so caught up in their own struggles, their own regrets, that they couldn't see what was happening to me."

Eleanor nodded slowly, her face gentle. "Sometimes, child, we get so wrapped up in our own pain that we forget to see the pain of others. But it doesn't mean they love us any less. It just means they're struggling too."

Lilly's eyes began to well up with tears, but this time, they weren't from anger or frustration. They were from understanding. "I always thought they didn't care… that they didn't understand me. But now I see they've been struggling, just like I have. Maybe they didn't know how to help me, but they were doing their best in their own way. And I… I gave up on them too soon."

Eleanor reached out and gently placed her hand on Lilly's shoulder. "You're a strong girl, Lilly. You've been through a lot. But the hardest part isn't just surviving. It's learning to give others the grace they deserve, even when they can't give it to you right away. Sometimes, people are doing the best they can, even if they don't show it. Your parents love you. They just don't always know how to show it."

Lilly took a deep breath, feeling the weight of her realization settle into her chest. She could feel a shift inside her—a change in perspective. She hadn't understood before, but now she did. Her parents, just like Eleanor, had their own battles. They were imperfect, but they weren't bad people. They just hadn't known how to help her, the way she hadn't known how to help herself.

"I need to be patient," Lilly said softly, more to herself than anyone else. "I need to be patient with them. And with myself. I can't keep expecting them to fix everything. I need to be brave enough to handle it, even when they can't."

Eleanor gave her a soft smile. "That's the first step, Lilly. Realizing that healing takes time—not just for you, but for everyone around you. You're growing. You're learning to face your pain, and that's what will help you move forward."

Lilly nodded, wiping away the last of her tears. She felt a new sense of resolve building inside her. "I don't want to be like you, Eleanor. I don't want to give up on them, even when they can't be there for me. I don't want to leave them in their struggles, thinking I don't need them anymore. I'll be patient. I'll give them a chance to understand me, and I'll start by showing them that I understand them."

Eleanor's eyes softened as she gazed at Lilly, pride shining in them. "You're a wise soul, Lilly. You'll find your way. And when you do, you'll be stronger than ever."

Lilly smiled through her tears, her heart finally beginning to heal. The nightmare of Buddy, the confusion, and the pain—it was all starting to make sense. She wasn't alone. She never had been. And now, for the first time in a long time, she felt ready to face her parents, ready to face the future, ready to forgive everybody and ready to heal.

As the sun rose, she packed her bag and got ready to head home.